GRISELDA BLANCO
THE COCAÏNE QUEEN

AT THE PRICE OF BLOOD

STORY 3

Henri DAUBER

SUMMARY

PROLOGUE

Coca Leaf was used by Indians for centuries for its stimulating and soothing virtues in the form of tea or, simply, by chewing the leaves to extract the sap. In 1855, the German chemist Friedrich Gaedcke, crystallized her and obtained crystals which he named "erythtoxyline". A few years later, another chemist, Austrian this one, Albert Niemann, isolated the active principles of the Coca Leaf and discovered the anesthetic virtues. Hoechst laboratories did the Benzocaine. It was then used in the treatment of respiratory and eye diseases to anesthetize patients. But it was in 1865 that the physiologist, Wilhem Lossen, which resumed in the study after the death of Niemman, establishes the psychoactive properties of Coca.

Yet the great Sigmund Freud himself, strongly advocated its use to treat certain disorders, gastric and neurasthenic, but also advised its use because he was aphrodisiac. Therefore, it became popular and was incorporated in cigars, cigarettes and even chewing gum. But its virtues were so prominent that it made wine to Coca before making a soft drink, very popular for Americans before invading the world.

In France, we found cocaïne in 1871 in a wine very well known at that time: the wine Mariani, of the name of the pharmacist who invented the recipe, Angelo Mariani. His pharmacy, located Boulevard Haussmann in Paris, was not always full. And the buyers did not content themselves with only mixture made by wine of Bordeaux mixed with extract of Coca. They also bought pastilles from the cocaine, leaves to brew, and elixirs to take advantage of its stimulating qualities. Its most famous consumer were Thomas Edison, Jules Verne, and Emile Zola.

It was necessary to wait 1914 for the members of the United States regulate its use and limit the distribution with the Harrison Act. Now, Cocaine will be reserved for medical use. But its virtues continued to feed some desires.

In 1980, Americans sniffed 200 tons of cocaine. Pablo Escobar provided half of this consumption after building giant laboratories in the Colombian jungle. These laboratories were producing 10 tons of cocaine per week. At 5,000 dollars of profit per kilogram, he won this year that $ 5 billion.

The Medellin cartel, him, was born in March 1981. It consisted of 12 heads, in fact 12 bigger Colombian drug traffickers.

In 1985, Forbes magazine, in its section of the largest fortunes of the world, revealed that Pablo Escobar was the 7th largest fortune of the world. In the same ranking, three other traffickers from the Medellin cartel were part of the 20 biggest fortunes.

CHILDHOOD

The city of Medellin was the capital of the Department of Antioquia. She was in the Valley of the Aburrá Valley between the Cordillera Central and Western. The town was located at an altitude of 1538 meters, had earned him the nickname capital of the mountain.

The Spanish landed in this region at the beginning of the 16th century. The area was inhabited by indigenous people of different ethnicities. And as the region was rich in gold mines, the conquerors settled there. The first name given to the city was " Aburra de los Yamesies ", then "San Lorenzo de Aburrá" and "Valle de San Bartolomé", and finally "Villa of the Candelaria of Medellín", because most of the Spanish conquerors and the first Governor of the city came from the city of Medellin, small town in the Spanish region of Extremadura. But it was in 1674 she took its final name, given by the Regent Marie-Anne of Austria: «Villa of Nuestra Señora de Medellín»

She was the second largest city of Colombia thanks to its gold production, which represented 70% of the national production. But its economic development was through by its textile industry. The economic weight of this sector was an important center of fashion. Its inhabitants, the "Medellinense", were called "Paisas" by the inhabitants of the capital, Bogota, who so wanted to denigrate the population of this provincial town. Residents did pride and then eventually call themselves proudly of this nickname.

The region had a humid climate where the temperature was between fifteen and twenty-five degrees. Many farms there emerged so, especially on the hills surrounding the town, which had earned the city of Medellin the nickname of "city of the eternal spring ".

But despite this wealth, most of the inhabitants were living in miserable conditions. And those who wanted a better future had for solution only to emigrate.

It was as well as Ana Lucia Restrepo manages to convince Roberto Blanco, the man she had married in a small church of Medellin, to leave this provincial town without future to try to build their lives in Cartagena, capital of Bolivar department. She had convinced him to go and live in this port city on the edge of the sea of the Caribbean, that we said rich. In this city were a maritime industry and a large petrochemical industry working at full capacity because of the second world war.

Yet, his family him her advised not strongly. Weren't happy in their small town of Medellin? So why leave?

It is true that since the Bible and the reputation of Sodom and Gomorrah, the city was known as dangerous and warned, in the image of the vile human appetites. But for those seeking a better life, she represented an area of freedom, refinement where dreams could be fulfilled through hard work and courage.

They were not disappointed when arriving in this city. They were even amazed by this city with the ancient fortifications that were part of the oldest of South America. The old city had eleven kilometers of walls erected by the Spanish to protect themselves from pirates who roaming, at this time, the sea of the Caribbean. Cartagena was the main port of the region where the gold was sent to Spain, to be used to buy slaves and goods. The slaves of Central America entered it as the gold went out of it.

The historic center of Cartagena was a strong attraction for those visiting her. Its balconies collapsing under bougainvilleas were the soul of the city, the cobbled streets, the castle of San Felipe, and its old baroque churches are sealed are sheltered under the old walls. It was in the former convent of the Poor Clares that Gabriel García Márquez, came as a journalist for the daily newspaper "El Universal", had found inspiration in speaking of the poor Servia Maria de Todos los Angeles in his book "love and other demons. He was then inspired by by the flavor of the centuries crossed as writing his biggest work, "One hundred years of solitude", book enabled him to win the Nobel Prize of literature. When the day was setting, sea breeze cooled off the air and Sun turned the colors of the facades of the old houses, be they Blue-King, butter-fresh or Sienna. Travelers said that she was a cousin of Havana, in Cuba, or of Salvador of Bahia, in Brazil.

With the swept away some savings, the young couple moved into a small pension that someone had recommended them. The house with thick walls stone brought freshness, augmented by the fountain located in the center of the patio. They now had to find job before their savings dwindle. In the meantime, they took the time to discover the city. They are kindred in different neighborhoods, sometimes asking restaurant owners or for bosses of bar if they did not look of the staff. We directed them to neighborhoods more animated when the need for staff was more important. Then in the evening, they were going on "Plaza de los coches", taking the opportunity to listen to musicians who played the "Cumbia", this local music that paid homage to the thousands of slaves arrived by boat to be sold, where many went on the place Simon Bolivar, the place where many people came to soak up the festive mood of the neighborhood.

It was said that Cartagena was Indian, creole and Spanish at the same time. The perfect city for Roberto, the black man, and to Ana Lucia, the white girl. In fact, the coat of arms adopted by the Republicans at their independence in 1811, was an Indian sitting in the shade of a Palm tree, the standard-bearer on the back, a grenade in his right hand, his left hand clutching a bow and his left foot trampling a broken chain, sign of the newfound freedom.

The two young lovers appreciated as sunsets than air dirty and iodine from sunrise of the day. When they were walking in the morning in the streets, they loved the interlacing of the alleys and the Palace of Andalusian type at the corners of the Plazas, these small places where the people sat down to enjoy a cool drink or a ice cream. It was the best time to discover the riches of this city, until the heat invaded it. The streets were built narrow to protect themselves from it. Besides when the Sun was pointing at noon, balconies gave a sufficient shadow to be immune to the bites of the Sun.

This city, founded in 1533 by Pedro Heredia, Spanish conquistador who settled there after discovering many graves of Indian chiefs met gold, had an ideal strategic position on the Caribbean Sea. She became an important port where African slaves purchased with gold stolen from the Indian Incas and Aztecs arrived. And the Quint, the twentieth, went by boat to Spain. His wealth made her an economic stronghold of the Spanish realm and attracted a large number of personalities, making her play a key role of the Spanish Empire in South America. The port was fortified to protect against pirates who roaming in the Caribbean Sea, and held a prominent place in maritime trade between the Spain and its colonies. But time passed and things changed.

After the invasion of Spain by the Napoleonic armies, Cartagena born the first Colombian insurgent outbreaks against the Spanish realm. As a result of Caracas and Buenos Aires, a first junta was established in the city on June 14, 1810. But it was necessary to wait until November 11, 1811 the province's independence is declared. Other provinces followed and a first Congress took place on 27 November in Tunja. Officials adopted the Act of the Federation of the United Provinces of New Granada, and decreed the independence. But the Spanish, not decided to let, reacted violently. A young general, Simon Bolivar, began at the service of the Patriots of Cartagena and fought against the Spanish forces.

Between December 23, 1812, and 10 January 10, 1813, Bolívar liberated towns on the Rio Magdalena and allowed the junction with the Patriots in the center of the country. December 12, 1814, he entered in Santa Fe of Bogotá, which became the capital of the new country. But the Spanish Royalist forces regained the upper hand and began a Reconquista, forcing him to flee in Jamaica. Cartagena fell on December 6, 1815, after three months of siege. Bolivar will call her "The Heroic" for its resistance. It will be necessary to wait until 1819 and the victory of Simon Bolívar to Boyacá so that Bogota found independence. But Cartagena, she, found her only on 10 October 1821.

And if the Colombia took the name of the discoverer of the continent, leaving to the neighboring country to that of Bolivar, these men marked forever, the spirit of those who ran the country.

Ana Lucia and Roberto eventually find a job. It was over there was born Griselda Blanco, their only daughter, February 15, 1943.

The father worked on the port, one of the oldest in the country. He loaded and unloaded the boats that did stop, to toil 12 hours a day to earn what is shelter and food. The mother, she, worked as a waitress in a "cantina", one of these cheap breweries where sailors came to eat, but also drink. And sometimes more than of reason.

The port workers, too, frequented too these places where we ate for cheap. Roberto, just like the guys who worked with him, used to come and eat in noon in the cantina where Ana Lucia worked. Not only for her beautiful eyes but because it allowed them to be well served. And as the lunch was often the only meal of the day, might as well eat to satiety.

But one day, a sailor, who had drunk too much, was too aggressive with Ana Lucia. Evil took him as Roberto was on hand to eat, too. He remained first of marble, waiting to see how far the man was ready to go. He was not afraid of the fight but because they had an hour for lunch, it was better not losing it in a quarrel. As this could have the consequence of making them loses their work both.

But the sailor continued and eventually goes too far. Much too far for his taste. Could not accept that this man lack of respect to his wife, he rose to interfere and it ended as he feared. The exchange of punches began between them two, until the one and the other companions don't get going in turn. Determined to beat this individual and his cronies, a brawl broke out. But it happened in the worst way. Roberto found himself lying on the ground, the skull opened by a bottle that he had broken on the head. At this sight, sailors fled immediately without asking their rest, sawing the blood that lay the head of one of their opponents. Alerted, Ana Lucia rushed with her husband to bring her aid. But his eyes, open, moved more.

"They killed him! They killed me! "She began to cry.

The blow on the head had been very strong. Too strong. Roberto had the skull smashed by the ass of the bottle of rum which had not broken upon impact.

The police was called to the rescue and would make an investigation to find the culprits, they did not find them. They were so satisfied to report more on a fight that took place on the port between the sailors who would stop and the people who worked there.

Nothing was able to calm Ana Lucia's sadness which made bury her husband as her was able to him. At least, as her means allowed it her. Roberto was placed in the ground and only a wooden plate allowed identifying the one which stood on this site.

He only had one more thing to do: go back from where she had left a few years earlier to return with her family. Cartagena was a beautiful place, the city would be more than the place where her husband had been snatched.

Ana Lucia and Griselda were restarted in reverse the National Road 25 which left from Cartagena and ended in Medellin.

Griselda, the little girl, was two years old.

But that still tiny, Griselda felt the difference between this rather poor provincial town, located in a high valley, and also cheerful city that joyful by the sea where she had made her first steps. People were more sad and much less welcoming. She realizes even more when, with her mother, she returned to the family home. The welcome they received was anything but jovial.

It was tradition in poor families live together and helps each other to improve. Ana Lucia had not respected this tradition and went with her husband to try an adventure elsewhere. So, when she stood in front of his parents, without husband and with a very young girl, they agreed to give her home that she finds work as quickly as possible and that she reverse half of what she won at her parents.

World War II had just ended and maybe food demand was going to increase, allowing agricultural companies of the region to work all those who were unemployed. But this was far from being the case.

So, in this city where labor would not run the streets, Ana Lucia decided to make the oldest profession in the world: the prostitution.

Although mother of a little girl, she was still young and appetizing enough to attract the gaze of men. She forgot her pride of wife and mother, drowning it in the alcohol vapors, merely saving money that would allow them to eat and to stay with her parents. She calmed his disgust in saying that this was only temporary. Besides, in the bars where she touted, she offered free her favors to the bosses to hope to be able to work as a waitress. And by dint of persistence, eventually it paid off. She found a job as waitress and reserved her generous forms for the only benefit to the boss who employed her.

The money was much less important. But he was much more moral. And to calm his mother torments, she explained to her daughter, who began to speak and so to ask questions, that life was much more than what fairy tales told.

"You know my daughter, we, women, we were designed by God to enlighten the world and to provide all the heat he needs. We are as a flame that burns without saying anything, without complaining, merely do what it was designed. We suffer, but we accept our fate, because we know that our flame gave light to those who wanted nothing and she has given the heat in the hearts of men who lack both.

-Mom, why men have no heat in their hearts?

-Because men are like this. They are hard and much more near the animals than gods. Once upon a time,

15

women were considered equal to gods, as goddesses. And then one day, Christianity arrived and decreased the role of women by limiting it to that of ownership of the men to make them, supposedly, pay Eve's fished.

-Who is Eve?

-Eve was the wife of Adam, the first man on Earth, created by God but who, supposedly, pushed Adam to eat the Apple that God asked to not eat.

-Why he ate then?

-Because he wanted to, simply. Adam didn't need Eve to eat the forbidden fruit. But the Church, which didn't blame Adam to have broken God, did carry all the blame on Eve. Since, we, women, we are condemned to work to fix this offense.

-And yet we did nothing, we?

-Not my daughter, we did nothing. But preachers have condemned us still for this so-called fished. And so we are obliged to respect certain moral virtues that we impose the Church but which allows men to do whatever they want. Virtue is the duty of the women and education that a mother must transmit to his daughter. »

Ana Lucia continued education of Griselda until she is old enough to enter the school.

COLOMBIA

When the president of the United States, James Monroe, decreed in 1823 "America for the Americans", he drew the contours of the expansionist policy of the United States who was to say to the European powers not to intervene on the American continent and to the new independent republics that their powerful neighbor was there to provide all assistance they might need. Their true purpose was to be the Hegemon within the continent.

In 1905, the president Theodore Roosevelt ushered in an era of aggressive relationships by applying "The big stick policy" which introduced the right for the United States to intervene anywhere on the continent, even without legal legitimacy, and against any Government, so democratic is.

So that after several military interventions, the majority of American nations condemned the interventionist policy of the United States during the American States Conference International in Havana. The First World War and the formation of the League of Nations, Ancestor of the United Nations Organization, calmed down things for a few years, United States having the look towards Europe. Especially since president Franklin Roosevelt tried, to improve good neighborly relations by breaking with the Monroe doctrine. The Second World War and the communist menace changed things.

In 1945, in Mexico, the Act of Chapultepec stipulated that "any surge of communism in America would be a victory for the Soviet Union". The witch hunt born in United States, which supported all American regimes, be they democratic or dictatorial, to combat the Red peril.

17

Diplomacy American came into play and resulted in the signature of the American Treaty of Mutual Assistance of Rio of Janeiro, December 2, 1947, stipulating that any armed attack against a American State would be considered an attack against the other American States. It became the first step towards the institutionalization of policy safe Pan-Americanism and was finalized on April 30, 1948, with the Charter of Bogota, who created the OAS, the Organization of American States, who promoted political, economic and cultural cooperation between all the States of the continent. It was the first layer of the sphere of influence of United States.

One of the consequences of this agreement was the exacerbation of tensions between the leaders of national political parties, opposing between the desire for independence for some and the submission to the big brother of the North for others. In Colombia, Liberals confronted with to the Conservatives. But it was not the first when both political currents clashed violently.

At the end of the 19th century already, Colombia experienced its largest civil war, Liberals opposed to the replacement of the constitution of 1886, decided by the Conservatives. It lasted from October 17, 1899 to November 21, 1902 and was called the thousand days war. Its consequence was the separation of the region of Panama in 1903, at the instigation of the Government of United States. The Conservatives took him and kept the power until 1930, date in which Liberals won the election and ruled until 1946. They eventually split and lost the presidential elections. The Conservatives, again to the legitimate power, had no majority in the Congress. They had to act.

This results in the assassination April 9, 1948 of the left-wing candidate, Jorge Eliecer Gaitán in Bogotá, near to the middle class and the poor, and favorite of the polls for the presidential election, after that his party won the municipal election in June 1947. This murder provoked riots in Bogota who was a crackdown and turned into a civil war, called "Violencia".

MEDELLIN

The Valley where the city of Medellin was built was discovered by Spanish in August 1541. These men had been sent on an expedition by Jeronimo Telejo to find land and riches. They discovered Indian villages, of different ethnicities, but belonging to the strain of the Indian Caribbean, and found the place to install settlers.

March 2, 1616, Francisco de Herrera Campuzano founded the village of "San Lorenzo de Aburrá". Other settlers arrived, and two centuries later, in 1813, the Governor declared her as a city of the fact of its commercial importance. On April 17, 1826, she was raised to the title of capital of the region of Antioquia. Temperatures ranged from 30 degrees in the day to 16 degrees at night, which earned him the nickname of "city of flowers and of eternal spring".

The conflict generated by "La Violencia" saw the emergence of conservative armed bands responsible for cleansing the country of Liberals. The membership of a village or a city to the liberal party them exposed to abuses by armed bands who did not hesitate to burn down them, shave them, after having killed its inhabitants and violated women. Militias of self-defense were formed to protect them. Families had as loopholes to escape to the mountains or to the jungle to escape of the devastating fury. It was a time of extreme violence that shook the Colombian mentality.

Medellin, the second city of the country, did not escape this violence.

TEENS

With this period of civil war, it seemed that all the inhabitants of the country had become crazy. This generation, propelled into the labyrinth of events and of the war, was sacrificed to this conflict that some named the Reason of State to better them to accept deprivation, of food and of freedom. The reaction of the youth was to forge his hatred and sharpen his tantrums to better cut the ties that restrained them. But it will eventually tear everything around them.

Ana Lucia had ended up losing his job. Both because his boss was tired of her favors but also because his daily consumption of alcohol had started to decay his beauty. It was things that were coming. But the worst was that she had not found another job and that she was now the only one in the family to work. His father was ill-health and had no money for treatment. He said that he expected only one thing, death come and faster she would come, better it would be.

It was therefore resolved is to engage in prostitution hoping to earn enough money to be able to provide the necessary care for his father. But despite his efforts, this had died after four months. She was catapulted as head of the family and had the responsibility to feed everyone. This was her destiny, she thought. Had it been another, she would have lost her husband because a sailor to wandering hands. Then to forget his woes, she increased his consumption of alcool.

Sometimes when she came home and her daughter, Griselda, did not sleep, she tried to answer his questions. Until the day where she asked her what she was doing as a profession.

"Since you were born, my daughter, I do the work I can find. And there is little work that is given to a woman. Then, I do the work that I do, even if it doesn't make me happy.

-There are some boys in my school who say that you're selling to men, she said.

-You know my daughter, we're three in home to eat. And it's just me who works and brings money to eat. So you tell these idiots that they take care of their business. And if they have something to tell me, that they come to me! »

This explanation had merit alone to stir his curiosity. Griselda did not fail to return on roses the boys who mocked her saying that her mother was only a girl of joy. They were still a little young to use the term of bitch.

But a few months later, she again asked the question to his mother because, this time, it was the mother of one of the girls in her class who had forbidden him to see her.

"You know my daughter, there is a greater misery than the condition of the people.

-Why, Mom?

-The poverty of the heart, my daughter. People think that a woman who is successful with men is a woman of easy virtue because she would sell her body for money. But a woman sells not more for the money that a married woman offers because it would have received a gift from her husband. It is the same thing except that a woman of easy virtue does voluntarily as does the married woman. The only difference is that the married woman does with her husband while we, women who like men, do so with men we want.

- And what's better, Mom, do with her husband or with other men?

-That, my daughter, you'll find when you get older. But if you must one day be ashamed of what other, think then you won't live for you, but you live to the eyes of others. Just know that you can decide yourself what is right and what is not. In any case, if men make you gifts, whether jewelry or money, take everything you can until the last peso! »

It was as well that Griselda was educated. Sometimes, her grandmother contradicted those words which she felt was disproportionate and inappropriate for a child. She was the counterweight to his mother who, because she was forced to prostitute herself and by the alcohol she consumed in unreasonable quantities, was inconceivable remarks for the education of a girl.

But like his grandfather, her grandmother eventually dies. Griselda was eight years old. The emotional trauma she suffered the loss of one who truly cared for her was that she approved more the words of his mother.

One evening, she questioned her about the morality.

"In the world we live, my daughter, to know that a woman's place is expected to serve men. Men consider themselves as superior to women and do consider us as objects meant to serve or satisfy them. Whether it's mundane requests or requests more vulgar.

-Men are so bad?

-This isn't wickedness, my daughter. Men are human beings primaries. A stupid man will consider a woman as a simple object without taking the trouble to consider a woman newsworthy. This is our environment that wants it. Maybe in the big world, things are different. But when I see what are capable people who manages this country, I don't think they are better. »

Because the civil war continued and the massacres were did not stop. The Conservatives remained in power and continued their armed struggle against Liberals. The war lasted until June 1953, when the general Rojas Pinilla organized a Coup to take power and put an end to the bloodbath which did not stop. Flickering democracy was replaced by a military power strong which put an end to the fighting and allowed a gradual return to normality. Pockets of resistance continued but the general enacted an amnesty law for those who laid down the weapons. Peace was returning.

Griselda was ten years old. She made acquaintance with the throes of femininity. She didn't know what this was and knew that his mother was the only person who can explain this. Even if she did it his way.

"It means that you become a woman, my daughter. Even if you're still just a child.

-A woman. But I have only ten years old, mother!

-After what the preachers, we inherited this Eve...

-Her again!

-Yes my daughter, all comes from Eve. Don't forget that she was the first woman.

- And we have already, this Eve?

-When a girl becomes a woman, she discovers her first menstrual rules. These rules come back monthly thereafter and repeat until the day where a woman can no longer have children.

- And it lasts long, mother?

-A week, my daughter. During this week, you'll lose some blood and you have severe pain in the stomach. But worry my daughter, all women know that. It ends only when the woman is pregnant and she is expecting a child. And when she gives birth, then, she knows well most strong pain.

-You hurt that, mother?

-Yes my daughter, women are made to suffer. All because God told Eve, she will give birth in pain!

-Still because of her?

-No, not her daughter, because of God! »

Ana Lucia was invaded by a strange feeling. His daughter became wife. She had not seen him grow up or had not realized that her daughter was a teenager. What would make about her? Should she continue to go to school or well should she explain to him that it was time to learn a trade to be able to work and earn a living? She was tortured but said that she was now a young girl and that it could be useful and brings it as money at home. To allow him to have the money to buy the alcohol that she persevered in increasingly unreasonable amount. She drank a swig from the bottle of alcohol that she held in the hands and said she would think before you sink into the alcohol vapors.

It was at this time that she met Joaquim, a bad boy in his neighborhood. Joaquim was part of a gang who paced the streets of Medellin and was the pockets of some customers. And the boy was endowed. So endowed that he ends up becoming the leader of this small band. Griselda became the girlfriend of the head and began to assert himself. She said that she became his mistress while she was barely eleven years. It worked perfectly until the day where Joaquim was set in obvious offence of robbery. Direction prison for adolescents. Hell, in sum.

But Griselda withstood the shock. In fact, it was not the first that she was living in her young life. She takes the bad news. His heart had become hard for a girl of her age. She had to make that to what his mother had put him through without his knowledge. Because it happened that his mother became an alcoholic to endure the rigors of prostitution, sometimes mixed powdered milk with alcohol instead of just water. She did it unwittingly, under the influence of alcohol, and when sometimes the grandmother would find out, she replied her was better she drinks firewater instead plain water "to prevent childhood diseases".

Griselda therefore took over from Joaquim. But she was a woman and had to use his fists to get respect. This

26

seemed to work until the day where one of the members of the band wanted to oppose her. She got rid of him planting a knife in the stomach.

"You think it's because I'm a girl you're going to send me? She spat him in the face, even surprised by his determination to have managed to get the upper hand.

- Forgiveness, Griselda, forgiveness, muttered the boy of thirteen. I didn't know you'd be so strong. Now, I respect you and I never do it again, I swear.

-So, you listen to me! And you others too! She spoke out loud to the other boys. In the absence of Joaquim, it's me who runs the band. This idiot thought that I won't be at the height. Evil took him. He's just lucky I didn't kill him. Otherwise, I would have planted the blade in the heart. But the next will not have this chance! »

From this day forward, nobody of the band disputed his authority. Thinking back to what his mother often told him: "In the world where we live, my daughter, to know that a woman's place is expected to serve men because men see themselves as superior to women."

She began to organize the band and defines the areas where needed to operate. She establishes who reported the most money, those where the risks were most important and the best way to operate. Either alone, or in small groups, or to be acting as grasshoppers when they ransack a field. Once this set up, she decided to give a name to their band. It would be called the "Debiluchos", the weak, to the chagrin of its members who understood not interest to give such a name to a band. They far preferred

27

to call themselves the "Lords", the "Kings" or another name well more peremptory. But when Griselda tried to explain to these ignorant the benefit of such a name, she became disenchanted before their stupidity. These boys were really good to fill the menial. It was really not with them that she would accomplish great things.

Months went by and she began to bring some money to home that she gave to her mother who had more and more trouble to find customers. The reason was his excessive consumption of alcohol, which had begun to make him lose a few teeth.

Ana Lucia was more than a shadow of her former self. She had lost her pretty face and her smile, was more than all taste for life and not be tied only because she still felt responsible for her daughter who she had some form of admiration. Griselda, she, had dropped out of school but didn't matter it because it wasn't in this kind of place that we learned the life. In school you learned to read and write and once that was done, she was no longer anything else to people of their condition. Griselda understood this. She made the effort to stay a little longer because she wanted to know how to count, but as soon as it seemed more useful to him, she deserted school benches to join those where hanging Joaquim and his acolytes, who by far preferred the hard school of the street.

However, Ana Lucia began to worry that her daughter brings him money. She asked him where it came from but Griselda reassured her telling him that it was honestly earned money.

"Honestly earned? Asked the mother who knew that in the hills of Medellin, there were very few people who earned their money honestly.

-I'm telling Mom, it's money that I do not steal!

-I know how hard it is to earn his living honestly, my daughter. I do not blame you to win money. Us, women from a poor background, we know that the virtues do exist for those who do not know hunger. For us, they serve to be sold at the offering, hoping he'll give us the best price. I've worked hard, you know my daughter to feed you every day. And whatever you think of me, know that I did what I could to do to fill your hunger.

-I know Mom. That's why I bring you this money. Because it's my turn to enable you to have a little more comfort.

-I would never ask you what you're doing to earn this money, but I know that men are never good for us. Except to bring them pleasure! I want you to know also that I will never do you any reproach and that never I won't carried away by any morality. »

Ana Lucia was put in mind that his daughter had followed his example and engaged in prostitution. She had often spoken of the flame that burned without a guess its importance but who brought light and warmth. She saw her daughter like a moth, attracted by the light and heat of the flame, but that would eventually burn the wings, like her, had she done.

Griselda began to win his first bundles of pesos. The members of his band walked away, obeying his orders at the same time as they were relieved to have found a new leader and because decisions of the "Madre" allowed them to win even more money while taking less risk. This girl was a literate warrior. She was the only member of the band to read newspapers. All because she was interested in what was written for fishing ideas.

It was in one of her readings, she discovered that the son of an industrialist was kidnapped and the kidnappers had freed him against a large ransom. The thugs who had committed this crime had continued and will were specialized in kidnapping of children of wealthy people. This information gave him an idea that went into his fertile mind to not to leave. She began to dig the idea to make the same.

There was some middle-class persons who led a far more comfortable than their existence in their neighborhood. These people were simple traders which, for her, were enriching themselves by taking advantage that the residents could buy food only at home. It was also, she said to herself, because of them that his mother sank into alcoholism. She found it disgusting and began leading to punish them pulling allowing them to exercise their contempt in the face of the poor: money.

She went in all the little shops in his neighborhood and began to familiarize themselves with the faces and the habits of their owners. She uttered even follow some up to their homes. After a few days of investigation, she sketched her plan. But above all, he needed a gun, thing more of a deterrent than any knife. She managed to buy one to a man who worked as a pimp and who was using this ground of defence to protect his "girls" and getting respect from them.

"You want a gun? He asked her with pretension. And you want to do with it? It's not a toy, small girl!

-I have money to pay if you want to sell me one! She answered without taking into account what he had told her.

-Then give me five hundred thousand pesos and I'll bring it back!

-You think I'm going to give the money before? She addressed a smile to the lips.

-If you don't have confidence, then go to hell, small girl!

-Show me the gun and I'll bring you money! »

The man reflected a few moments and showed him the gun that he had on him.

"It will be the same as this one! Five hundred thousand pesos, don't forget!

-I'll take you in an hour. But I will not alone. If you ever want to rip me off, my friends will take care of you! »

She thought back to what his mother had taught him: "men think they are superior to women. Don't ever forget that. »

Griselda came back thirty minutes later. She was suspicious of this madman and expects what he tends a trap. Also, when the man arrived, the members of his band were stationed around the meeting place.

"You're already here, small girl? He asked her.

-You got the gun? She contented herself with say.

-Look small girl! »

She couldn't stand what they call it this way, sign of this spirit of superiority, but said that it was time to negotiate. And nothing else.

She approached and asked to see the gun. She took it in hand and felt a sense of power as she had ever felt.

"There are how many bullets in the charger?

-Fifteen! It should be enough for you, no?

-That's enough for now! »

She should not be intimidated and showed his determination. It was, she knew, the only way to be taken seriously. She handed him a wad of cash.

"Five hundred thousand pesos! And if I need another one, you will make for me a price? She began to bait him.

-It's already a good price!

-So we'll see! " She concludes.

She walked a few steps without turning the back and made a sign to the members of his gang to appear. A dozen boys went out on another, causing a grin of surprise to the man who had not noticed anything. He is then said he had done well to settle for doing business without trying to scam this girl of eleven. Eleven years and already bold. It promised.

Griselda explained his plan to the members of his clan. She had spotted his target and said that with the money that they scats, they would have enough to last many days without having to continue to take the risks they were taking in their activities of pickpockets.

Two boys followed their target when he went out of the school. They waited for the best moment to intervene and threatened him with their knives to force him to follow them. They took the boy in an abandoned garage and gagged him to stop him from screaming. As soon as this was done, two others surrendered in the trade of the parents and filed a letter to the counter, get going running as soon as it was done. The owner opened the folded sheet, and read what was written: if he wanted to see his son alive, he had to drop within two hours five million pesos to the address indicated.

The man was caught between two feelings: anger and despair. Five million pesos. It was a large sum but not enough to compare with the life of his son. He closed his store and took the money that was in the Fund. There was not enough. He went to his reserve, opened the small safe where he kept his recipe, and completed the sum. He put everyone in an envelope and went out through the back door to get to the address indicated in the letter. Once there, he had to wait. A boy came to talk to him and told him that his son was fine and that he would continue to thrive as long as he would not notify the police. The man handed him the envelope but the boy raised his hands, making him understand that he wanted nothing, and went away.

The father waited an hour in, looking right and left, and wondering what to expect and why we did wait. A motorcycle approached and stopped in front of him. Two boys were sitting on it and one of them, the gagged face, spoke to him.

"Give me the envelope, quick! " He shouted.

The father handed the envelope and received a kick to force him to back down.

"Your son will be brought in front of your store! Cried the boy again until the bike goes away.

The father then began to run, but not behind the bike. He returned to speed at his store, hoping to find his son. He was a few meters from the place, walking to catch his breath when he saw two boys who brought his son. He began to run, breathable jerkily, and took his son in arms when he was at its height. The boy was dazed but was doing well. He had nothing understood what had happened but was happy to find his father.

"We're going home", addressed the father to his son.

The son was left with the mother who was caught of nervous convulsions when the father explained to her what had happened. He asked her to lock the door of the apartment and went to the police station to inform the police of what was happened. He tried to give information, but the only one who seemed to be admissible was the profile of the boy who talked to him on the meeting place.

On their side, the strip of the "Debiluchos" celebrated their success through a bottle of brandy. Griselda was the only to settle for a beer. She couldn't bring herself to drink what had made her dependent mother at the point of destroying himself.

"It's our first success and given the speed at which the trader has brought money, means that the ransom was not important enough. Next time, be asked ten million pesos." She explained to these weak minds that made up his band.

The next day, they withdrew to the action. This time, it was the son of another shopkeeper. How to make was identical. Only the place where the boy was locked up was different. They were wary of prying eyes and did not want to take the risk of being denounced by neighbors.

The victim's father winced when he discovered the amount of the ransom: ten million pesos. He could not raise the money after a few hours and went instead of date that night had already fallen.

Griselda was wary this late but she knew, thanks to the boys that she had posted near the store, that the father had not gone to the police station to inform the police. He may be done by phone, but there was no indication that the police were on their trail. The father waited and saw two motorcycles to him. Instinctively, he drew back for fear of being the target of thugs but when the first motorcycle stopped in front of him, he took a step toward them.

"You got money? Asked the driver, a scarf over the face.

-Yes, I have the money, he replied.

-Then give it to those who follow me! "

He started immediately without giving him time to react.

The second bike approached and this one who stood behind the driver snatched the envelope of the hands, swinging him a kick to knock it down. The driver immediately gave gas and walked away. The man stood and saw the first bike back to him.

"Your son will be brought back home. You better that there be no police or get him his account! "

The man went home, so plagued by fear and tears. A few meters from his home, he saw his son sitting on the floor, hands tied in the back. He raised, detached him and clasped strongly in his arms.

"Come on, son, we're home!"

The next day, he did not open his shop and went to the police station. The police explained to him the same mishap happened to another merchant and that they would, today, around all the shops to warn the owners. Apparently, a bunch of young offenders had decided to shake down merchants in the neighborhood.

But the band of Griselda was faster than the police. She removed another boy and recovered ten other million pesos. Everything seemed to be happening for the better. The case seemed to turn out good, there was more than to widen the circle of traders to find other "clients".

But Griselda, who had noticed that the police were becoming worrisome, decided to go back to the first boy to have been removed.

"Your father has reported us to the police, she explained to the boy. So to punish him, he will have to pay a new ransom! »

But you had to be of the most cautious because police officers were on the teeth. As the father was, this time, decided not to pay, relying on the police to find his son.

The day after the kidnapping, a ransom had not been paid. Griselda sent one of his members of his band to try to get in touch with the parents. But the boy returned panic.

"There a lot of cops who swarm around the home of parents, he said. There is no way to approach them!

-It's over! Launched another.

-So what, Griselda? Asked a third.

-I'm thinking! "She answered them.

Things were not exactly as she wanted him. Not only this fool had told the police, but in addition he did not have to pay the ransom.

The next day, the boy seemed to become an unnecessary weight. He had to know what to do with him. Release him, and take the risk that this new business falls into the water, or show their determination so that others understand that they were ready for anything. She decided to call itself the parents. She went into a phone booth away from the district, searched for the phone number in a directory and called.

"Sir, you decided to not pay in exchange for the life of your son, she said taking a boy's voice. I warn you that if tonight you don't bring us ten million pesos, I will kill your son. So, many think that you do! "

She hung up and walked away from the place if the police would have spotted his appeal. She was sure that they had listened to the conversation. So as a precaution, she walked quickly away.

Parents hesitated in front of the threat, but police explained to them it was the second time that their son was kidnapped and ransom had increased. If they paid, they

37

would face that their son is kidnapped again. For them, should give no credit to what had been said. The police thought that the band that committed these crimes was only composed of teenagers and, for them, they wouldn't risk killing a young innocent boy.

Parents were convincing. Also, when the phone rang at night, the father told the correspondent that he would pay no ransom. He had paid once, but refused to give in this time. On the advice of the police, he proposed to the kidnapper to come get her son back himself to prove to them that he had no grudge against them. The phone was hung up by the one who had called. "Was-it a good sign? " He asked the police. These sought to reassure him, telling him that his determination would the kidnappers at the foot of the wall and they wouldn't have as outcome but to release his son. But the police did not know, was that Griselda saw things differently.

She spurred an angry as she had never stolen. His band members discovered a girl as they had never seen. They were tiny, lest she calms his nerves on one of them. And they saw something that amazed them. Griselda took his gun, took a bullet in the barrel, approached the boy, lying on an old stained mattress, and he lodged a bullet in the head.

"Don't need us you because your parents love you less than their money", she said out loud, as to excuse his crime.

The other members of the band jumped when the shot slammed.

"Now they will know all they have interest to pay. She threw to the members of his band.

-The police are going to come after us! Cried one of the boys, panicked.

-Shut up! Shrieked by threatening his weapon. It is normal to us to respect! - She breathed strokes to regain his composure and spoke to his acolytes - let's stop this activity time that police officers should be discreet. Each goes home and we find ourselves in two days. Date, place Bolivar! »

She wore his gun, took a few business and walked away, leaving his "Debiluchos' awe, still in prey to panic before the crazy move she had to commit.

Griselda knew that the crazy move she had to commit came to end, not this activity that seemed interesting, but he had also put an end to his band. She knew none of these weak minds would never come back. At the same time because they were afraid of being accused of the crime but also because they had discovered that their leader was ready to make anything to carry out its business. They obeyed him already on the finger and to the eye because they knew that the slightest indiscretion, they risked a penalty. They had already seen what she was capable of when she was took over from Joaquim. And now that she had a gun, she was even worse. More so than tonight, they had discovered that she would not hesitate to use it. This girl was crazy and she would train them in their madness.

Griselda went even when two days later on the Bolivar place. Just to check that she was not mistaken. As she was doubted it, any member of the band had come.

This well confirmed the end of the band of "Debiluchos".
"Too bad for them after all" she said to herself.

But he now had to find an activity that allows him to live.

FIRST LOVE

Griselda had left with with the ransom money. She had to keep some time but the money spent his mother in the drink would quickly deplete this source.

She started to ask her mother to drink less and chided him for his excessive consumption. Her mother's response was disproportionate.

"For whom do you think yourself, my mother?

-I'm worried about you, Mom. You should stop drinking this brandy.

-Take care of your affairs, silly little girl! " Threw by making a gesture that left no doubt about the intent.

It was the first time that his mother raised his hand on her. It was a sign. Griselda, who didn't used to be martyred, wanted to react. Both women fought as scavengers and, for the first time, she took a beating. Was it because she was stronger than her or because she had hesitated to strike his mother? The following days, the nature of their relationship gave the answer.

"I know you have money, Griselda. Go and buy me a bottle and do not delay! Ordered the mother.

-I won't, Mom. If you want to buy alcohol, you have to go there yourself! "

They fought themselves again, and once again, the mother took over. And this time, Ana Lucia was carried away by anger.

"You think you're going to make what you want at home, little fool you are! You're going to have to understand who is the mistress in this house! "

She continued so for long minutes and accompanied his every word of fists. The slaps were not enough to his liking, so she replaced them with fists. It was as well that Griselda bowed to his mother, yielding to the beatings that she began to administer, sometimes, without reason.

And what had to happen, happened. His mother, more cozy by alcohol, was more difficult to find clients. One day, prey to lack caused by absence of alcohol, she began leading to launch his daughter in this activity. Although she already wondered where she was shooting the pesos that she had brought back several months. She became convinced that it was an activity she probably already practiced.

One day, Ana Lucia brought back a client at home. It was time, because it had been several days that she had more them back. But this customer came for another reason.

"This is my daughter, said Ana Lucia. Look how pretty she is! "

The 30 year-old man approached Griselda, sitting on a Chair, touched her hair, then her cheek and looked at the mother.

"Three hundred thousand pesos? He asked her.

-Three hundred thousand, Yes! "

Man stood up, walked out of notes for ten thousand pesos, counted and handed them to Ana Lucia, who showed him the room. The man took Griselda by the hand, forced her to get out of his chair as the girl saw the reason, and pulled until the curtain which served as the gateway.

Ana Lucia had many misfortunes in her life. Misfortunes she had been able to endure and which had led him to the doors of alcoholism. But this time, she became there is worst in a mother: prostitute her child.

It often happened that the girls follow the path of their mother. When she was a prostitute and this activity was to support the family, she became an easy way to get money. Sell her body. The oldest profession in the world. But also the most vile.

Griselda was going on twelve years. She found itself in a bed with a man three times as old as her. Needless to say, the shock that the young girl undergoes. She knew nothing about the men. She had been so far for only lover that fasting Joaquim, she loved and to whom she was offered willingly, offering him her virginity. But Joaquim was only two years older than she. What she discovered, that day was the anatomy of one man over thirty years. A chubby man, the face bloated and hairy to the shoulders. And the worst was when he undressed. She discovered his sex in erection and a pocket quite wrinkled underneath, which rocked in each of the movements. As Joaquim was a beautiful stallion with fair skin, as this man looked like a hairy bear.

The man forced her to give in to all his demands. Then she discovered the sexual act, For lack of act of love. But she endured without shouting. Because when you cried, we lost the way to express his disgust and contempt for those who committed this act. At first she had trouble but this will eventually fade, enduring the painful sensation.

43

And unbeknownst to him, his body began to gesticulate and to feel a form of pleasure, while the fat boy who rode her, emitted sounds, interrupted by noisy breathing. She felt the movements back and forth to accelerate, his body stiffen then, at the time the strongest, she felt like a fresh explosion in her. The man, him, succumbed to the pleasure, lengthened her whole being on her and moving more. "He's dead?" She wondered. No, unfortunately he was not. While she let herself go to a strange feeling of well-being, human rose, tempering this moment that resembled a kind of happiness. Involuntary happiness but happiness anyway.

The man went out of the room and spoke to Ana Lucia.

"You told me that your daughter was virgin?

-Of course her is! She replied.

-Liar! You get two hundred thousand pesos!

-You better give me three hundred thousand otherwise...

- Otherwise what! "

The man accompanied his words with a slap that sent her against the table.

"Two hundred thousand, is what you get! " He added before you leave the house.

She had lost one hundred thousand pesos. And all this because her daughter was not virgin.

"Little bitch! She cried before entering the room. Here, take this! "

She gave a beating to Griselda to make her pay the hundred thousand pesos that she had just lost but also for the slap she received because of her.

Not only the girl had to be taken by force by an uncouth, and pedophile of addition, but in addition she received a beating by his mother for all thank-you. Life took a turn as she had never thought to know.

The worst is that it was only the first time. His mother continued to prostitute her because she no longer had the physical allowing her to find customers. Things continued this way for years. It was the only way that found Ana Lucia to earn the money to buy the daily bottle of brandy that he needed to calm the tremors of his hands.

Griselda continued to undergo the prostitution imposed upon his mother and the beatings she gave her when the alcohol vapors had ravaged his brain and made her a beast. What the girl undergoes three years hardens her heart to make him dislike everything that represented the human species.

At the age of fourteen, she decided to no longer suffer the tempers her mother inflicted her. She had kept the gun she bought when she led the band of "Debiluchos" and decided, one day, putting it under the nose of her mother if she hit her. So that the day where it came, she took out his gun and stuck it under the eyes of this mother that she hated. His mother, took in a self-destructive madness, was not afraid to see the barrel of the revolver.

"You want to kill me, my daughter, then go ahead and kill me. Finish this once and for all. You think I'm afraid of death, and well you're wrong, my dear. Death, I call it my greeting every day since your father died. So go ahead and kill me and free me from this unworthy life! "

Griselda had not the courage to pull the trigger. Although her mother made her suffer the worst throes, she was her mother and knew how the poor woman had suffered. So that's why she persevered each day as to brandy. It was to shorten this miserable life was hers.

One day, she took her mother, drunk, falling down to the room take a few things and runs away from home. She did not know where to go, but didn't matter it the place where she would happen. Whatever it was, it couldn't be more terrible than the place where she had lived the past three years.

Griselda won half of the money she had saved to her mother. It was normal. It was she who did the "work", she has was sacrificed. That money, she deserved it. Much more than her mother.

She walked into a bar that she knew and who rented rooms. Even if these were used by prostitutes who commandeered the passers-by. She spoke to the boss who agreed to rent her a room. As long as she pays in advance. She paid the rent for a week, filed its affairs, locked the door, and headed outside. She peered the street and sought a place where she could settle for work. There were three girls who pounded the pavement. Not matter so to land and make them compete. She walked so sought a place where people spent and, above all, where no one was in place. The only place she found "suitable" was located near a park bench.

She moved there and waited. Little time because after ten minutes, a man stopped and started the discussion.

"One hundred thousand pesos and you pays the room! "

It amounted to one hundred and ten thousand pesos. The ten thousand extra pesos paid for the room would allow her to occupy her room free of charge. She had not warned the owner of the bar before making this decision but she knew, in advance, that he would not jib winning a little more than the payment that he had claimed her.

It was her first customer. And the beginning of a work she does for years. This prostitution activity allowed her to live. And even good live. Even if morality saw things differently. She thought of what her mother said: "Never let yourself guided by what people call morality. There is moral for those who do not know hunger." Besides whenever she thought of her mother, she is likely to visit her without her knowledge and deposited some money under her pillow. Failing her allow do not starve to death, because she knew she would deprive is easier to eat that drinking, that money would allow her to drown her pain of living in alcohol.

As if she had lived in total darkness for years, Griselda woke up from this nightmare on February 15, 1961. That day, she celebrated her eighteen years partying with some visiting friends and began a flirtation with a boy who seemed to have the heart, Carlos Trujillo.

The boy was twenty years old and worked as a mechanic in the only garage in the neighborhood. His specialty to him, it was the bikes. He knew that people came from other districts for asking him to fix their motorized gear. This form of successful immediately pleased him. It was a sign of quality, as trivial as it seemed. And then he looks simple, very simple, being interested in the girls more than that. It was a big contrast in terms of virtue and innocence, with her who was selling her charms and knew the consequences of a turbulent sex life. Yet despite these differences, the boy was interested in her, without taking into account the bad reputation she had.

During their first discussion, Carlos asked her what had caused him to have to prostitute itself. She told him her life and what she's going through on the part of her mother, an alcoholic and a prostitute. He immediately took empathy for her, before eventually succumb to his charms. He was the first man that Griselda brought in his bed without pay. It was a sign. And it was so, they continued their relationship. To the point that she decided to change at first place of resort, and then life. Carlos helped her find a waitress working in a bar. That was the condition to keep their relationship. She accepted it without hesitation. After all, she prostituted herself by obligation.

And after a few months of normal life, Carlos asked for her in marriage. Life took a nice turn and she would not deprive to live it in the best possible way.

They settled in a small apartment that became even smaller when she found herself pregnant, a few months later. She had a son which they called Dixon because Carlos likes this American name.

A year later, she gave birth to another boy, called this time Uber. Funny name for a Colombian. But once again, it was Carlos who chooses the first name. They did now more attention in their reports, the birth of two boys also close forced them to move, and it was not easy for her to balance her work at the bar with the education of her children. As the bad life she had known had encouraged her to put a point of honor to give them the essentials of education: a mother's love.

Life was perfect. Too perfect even for them who were from a very modest background. But the professional qualities of Carlos persuaded him to open his own garage. It was the beginning of a more comfortable life, although Carlos worked hard, very hard, to win money to support his family. Griselda had quit her job as a waitress at the request of her husband and the significant time he devoted to his bikes, began to become painful and source of tension. His nerves began to drop and many beers, because he liked American beer, offered by its customers, arranged not things. He returned home and more often later while intoxicated.

Griselda, who had already experienced this with her mother, was not prepared to bear again. So she began to blame him, further souring their relationship.

It calmed a time with the birth of their third child. Still a boy but, this time, it was she who chooses the first name: Osvaldo. Anyway, Carlos won't be was even bothered to go see her at the maternity. And worst of all, when she came home, she found a smell that was like nothing to what she knew. Carlos had taken advantage of his absence to bring another woman. How dared? He, the boy so sweet and so caring, how he could change so much?

It was true that Carlos was no longer a simple mechanic, a vulgar repairman of motorcycles to the combination full of oil stains. He became a garage owner.

And added to its qualities, he had become a person of interest. In addition to a woman interested. He needed to know more. Who was the woman who had slept with her husband? Was it a prostitute? She couldn't believe it. She knew what he thought of the women in prostitution and it was impossible that he could give to a woman in the street. The bitch that had soiled her sheets in the permeating smell had to be a client. So she decided to come and make a few visits to her husband with the children to find out who he was.

It was not long to Griselda to know who was the bitch. Without warning, Carlos had hired a secretary to take care of the paperwork of the garage. She came one day unexpectedly, and took that Carlos was busy chatting with a customer to enter the office. She had barely entered that she recognized the smell that had permeated his sheets. It was so she the bitch. She remained marble when the woman bowed to her and asked her what she wanted. Griselda hesitated before answering: should she make a scandal to her husband or pulling the hair of that whore?

She had no time to find an answer. Carlos had seen her and had come into the office quickly. The surprise of Griselda, he had a reaction that she would have imagined.

"What are you doing with the kids? He upbraided him.

-I came to see my darling, she said in a provocative tone.

-You come to me? And since when are you interested in what I make?

-Since you're late and you have a scent of a woman, that's why I'm here? "

Carlos, offended by these remarks and complaints that his wife made him in front of his secretary, took her by the arm and out of the office.

"Listen to me, Griselda. Here, the boss is me and I do not accept that you talk to me like that in front of my employees. Then you lower your where you go!

-Don't worry, I'm going! I leave you with your secretary. And you should tell him to less wearing perfume, it save I found his smell on you and in my sheets! "

Carlos sent him a slap as she had not received when she had left her mother's home. It was a clear sign that she had unmasked him.

"You should rather not come any more to annoy me in my garage if I refer you to the sidewalk where I found you! "

He had to make his choice. He would keep his secretary as mistress and she, would only have to take care of home, children and, above all, let him do what he wanted: his American beers and having sex with his secretary.

Griselda said bowing her head. What should do: accept this situation, and take the risk that one day her husband throws her out to settle down with his mistress, or leave her and end up homeless with three children to feed?

It was an eternal life. She would give itself time to make his decision but what she already knew, she would make him pay this betrayal when the time comes. In the meantime, he had, already, prepares his next life.

SECOND HUSBAND

Griselda returned home, took care of her children trying to hold back the tears that inundated her eyes. His world was crumbling.

An hour later, Carlos came in turn. She was surprised to see him go so soon. She suspected that this was a reason. In crossing the door of the apartment, he called to find out where she was. She did not answer. He walked with a purpose and found her in the bedroom, lying on the bed, near tears. No, not because of what he had done, but because she already knew he wasn't home for nothing.

"You're proud of yourself! He began to scream. You ridiculed me in front of my staff! And you think I will accept it! "

He threw himself on her and began to give her slaps banging whenever her palm touched the face. She only resisted him. Nevertheless, the desire never failed him yet she had decided how far he would go. And he went away. It was only when his nose began to bleed that he ceased his punches.

"You're going to take your stuff and you are going to go away from here! I take the kids to my mother and you better not be here when I get back! "He added to complete.

She did not dispute his decision. Yet, the pain of having withdrawn his children was unbearable to him. But she knew, have already experienced, that his children would be much better in this apartment they knew and they would have a better life than she could provide.

She waited that Carlos leaves the apartment to react. She went in the bathroom, cleaned his face to hunt the blood and rinsed itself in great waters to soothe the pain and try to recover. She returned to the room, took a large bag where she put a few affairs, then went into the dining room, opened a drawer of the cabinet where she had seen several times Carlos deposit money, took out a small wooden box, took all the notes that she found, closed it and put it back in the drawer. She took special care to leave the drawer open so that he realizes that she was not a party empty-handed. She opened the door and went out without looking back. The beautiful life she had had during four years had just ended.

Griselda returned to the bar where she worked before I met Carlos. Not only because she knew the place and she intended to resume the service, but also because she had hoped he would came find her back the money she took. But she was not gone with the money. She had also taken the gun bought there years and whom she had not discarded. Inside of her, she hoped that he come and give her the same fate. Not by masochism, but to pay him what he had made her. And in that kind of pain, the heart was much more painful than that of the body.

Fortunately and unfortunately, Carlos never came to claim the money. She received a visit; his mother-in-law, in charge of putting back to handing her an envelope. Inside was a divorce application. The woman explained that her son wanted full custody of the children, something that he would never, give her in exchange for the payment of a sum of money. Griselda signed the document less for money than for the good of his children. She knew the difficulties of life for a woman, then a mother with three children, it was even worse. And she couldn't help but think of her mother who had spent her life working as she could to feed, she and her grandparents. She knew that she would end up on the sidewalk. Unless you meet a man like Carlos once again. But knowing how things were over, she believed completely in love.

At the age of twenty-two, Griselda was a young woman with fresh complexion. The publican was not insensible to her charms and offered to hire her as a waitress. She knew in advance what would be the counterpart, but she accepted it and became his mistress. This liaison lasted a few months before he gets tired of her body. She resigned himself once more to accept his fate and decided to return to the pavement to prostitute itself.

She believed all the sincerity of men and felt unable to have, with any one of them, a relationship other than fee-based. His heart had dried up. She felt untied the less affectionate link, any tenderness and no longer lives in them than human beings just primary good to seek the pleasure of the flesh. She remembered again what her mother said of them: "Men see in women than just something good to serve their appetite, good to be consumed, delish a hole to be filled. Here's what most men see women. "

These thoughts moved her closer to her mother. And when the mother of Carlos came to give her money for agreeing to give him sole custody of the children, she took half money and returned to see her mother. It was the only person who had left and she wanted to know what she had become after eight years without seeing.

Ana Lucia had become a real mess. The body emaciated, alcohol and lack of food, a yellowed complexion which made her look like an old woman, while she was barely fifty years old. Her mother began to cry when she saw her get into her wretched apartment. Was it shame or happiness to see her daughter after all these years? Griselda put his hand in front of the mouth and nose to try and resist the foul smells that swamped her. It smelled of vomit, urinates, excrement, added to the body odor of her mother who had not to wash for weeks.

> "You can't just stand here, mother, she said, near to tears. I'll take you to the hospital for help, and when you're better, I'll take you with me. We live both as before. You want good mother? "

Her mother did not answer. She looked dazed, without saying a word. Griselda took the few cases that she found, slipped it into a plastic bag and forced her mother to get up from his bed. Ana Lucia walked as she could, being guided and almost carried away by his daughter. They walked for long minutes before arriving in a religious institution. Griselda knocked at the door, waited several minutes before someone doesn't open and proceeded to make the nun agrees to take her mother in charge.

> "It's the only parent I have and you only can get her out of her misery, my mother. I'll pay you the price will, but I beg of you, do what it takes to get her out of

alcohol. I know you did it with others and ask you to save my mom. "

She gave the religious how much money she had brought to her mother asking him to treat her well.

"I'll see her every week. If need you more money, my mother, I bring you!

-The money that you gave me will be enough for the moment, my daughter. What your mother has the most need is presence. We will take care of her. Just not seeing her for a month because the deprivation of alcohol will put her in a state of madness. We'll talk money at that time. "

Griselda got up, left the institution and returned to his occupations.

Two years ago she was hanging out in the same district, received his clients in the same room, which they were paying rent, and that the bar owner let as long as she accepts a few extras.

Then someday, as was the case with her first husband, Carlos, she met a man who seemed to be different from others. His name was Alberto and was driving a nice car, which earned him some success with some girls, ready for everything to fool around with this handsome who seemed to be a thug without seeming to. It was the case of all the girls in the neighborhood. All except one, Griselda. Contrary to the other girls, she knew to hide under a mask of impassive his feelings, that no man was also successful. And it was the lack of interest that she carried him that awoke the spirit of the young man, unaccustomed to what a girl interested in him. Because even if the men she met in her job didn't see that as an instrument of pleasure, Alberto looked her otherwise, finding in her a form of appeal, other than carnal interest. Before you succumb to his charm, she attempted to discern in him that hid this rogue side.

Griselda was twenty four years old when she yielded to Alberto Bravo. The boy appeared as tourism officer. He said he worked in a travel agency that was showing Colombia and Panama to American tourists. They were first knowledge, then taken to a mutual desire, became lovers. And as the pillow was the best place for confidences, he explained to her what his real job was.

Alberto was not all tourism officer or anything else. He was just a small smuggler who specializes in illegal immigration. He had worked well in tourism to Panama and Colombia, but not quite long to claim to be a tourism officer. He had made this job a few months before understanding that he would better his life playing guidebooks with Colombians, but only for those who wanted to visit United States of America. In fact, his job was to smuggle those who wanted to live in United States. And he knew the best way to achieve this.

Alberto fell in love with Griselda, who told him all his misfortunes with forms to soften her. He then tore from the street and offered to work with him. She hesitated, still dry heart and not yet ready to revive a love story. But as she could no more of this business of prostitute, she accepted his proposal to work with him. After all, even if their relationship would only last so long, it might find a way more moral, not to say most noble, to earn a living.

The two young lovers began to work together and thus doubled the circuits of delivery of illegal emigrants. The money which they won allowed them to settle in Bogota in a comfortable, for lack of luxurious. This was the first apartment where Griselda had a bathroom and a toilet private. It was almost a luxury for she who had never known it. But despite this, they were always that the 'paisa', bumpkins that people of the capital looked down on. Alberto, him, didn't care. He continued to roll in a nice car, at the expense of Griselda who couldn't stand women who turned in its path.

She was so afraid that her beautiful Hidalgo escapes him again. Then, she began to head to convince him to leave this cursed country where they would never be considered as bumpkins, that she be their success. She worked him, in the body at first, doing him things he had never known, maybe even ever seen in porn movies. She put weeks before convincing him that, ultimately, those who understood everything it was those who left to live in United States. And after weeks, he yielded to his proposal: Yes, they were going from them too, but before you let go, it was prudent to prepare for their departure. And the day where Griselda has waited the least he told him they were leaving them also.

The reasons for this shift were simple. He had counted money they had won and it was a small fortune: twenty thousand dollars. More importantly, he knew how to emigrates to United States and to settle to live unmolested by the North American authorities. He therefore proposed to leave and moved to New York. But first, he wanted to show his love by marrying her.

Griselda became Madame Bravo.

NEW YORK

Griselda and Alberto took a plane of the national company Avianca in Bogota to Panama City, their fortunes over them, because they didn't trust any of the people who worked at airports and that, sometimes, open the bags to retrieve valuables that were there. From Panama, they took another flight, of American Airlines this one, for New York. At the airport, they passed the customs without incident and took a taxi to the Borough of Queens. It was there that they settled and found even a job, but poorly paid work because they were only "chicanos". But it allowed them to touch as little as possible to their prize pool until we find better.

But while Griselda and Alberto spun the perfect love by taking advantage of their new existence, returns a spectrum: Carlos Trujillo. The former husband of Griselda. She fell from the clouds in seeing him one day while she was walking in the streets of Queens. How was it possible that this man, who she forget the existence, ended up here. She hesitated to talk to Alberto, but he noticed something was wrong with his wife for a few days. Then, she explained everything to him.

Alberto sought to know what had been able to bring this mechanic from Medellin to New York. He asked a few questions to people he knew for helping to immigrate to United States. One of them explained to him one day that Carlos Trujillo had been plucked by the girl who shared his life and that, after that she left with the cash to save his garage, he had contracted a loan to people who were engaged in smuggling. Unfortunately for him, he had been unable to honor its debt and had to cede his trade to its lender, which had threatened to smash the skull if he remained in Medellin. So he went to Bogotá where he was engaged into the smuggling of motorcycle parts to finance his departure from the country. He was two years old, he had landed in New York and started serving a bunch of Puerto Rican who provided security of traders against the payment of a tithe.

But it was a few months, the Chief of their band had been arrested by the police and Carlos then found himself at the head of this band which had eventually slapped some shops held by latinos. But the guy gave him information that would prove to be very important. Carlos had had the misfortune to shake down a latino bar which was under the protection of an Italian kingpin, whose one of the parents was member of Cosa Nostra. Carlos Trujillo had played with fire became too greedy. And he owed his chance to the large number of present Gunslingers in his band. So the kingpin was reluctant to tackle them and to expose themselves to a police response. For the moment, things were on stand by, but it was enough of a spark that blow.

Griselda learnt all this by Alberto and couldn't welcomed Carlos is strip by his Bimbo. It was what he deserved. But she worried for the fate of his three boys. She was convinced that they had remained in Colombia, near their grandmother, but not was not satisfied for all that. Maybe it was a sign of destiny. And a way for her to recover, finally, his three boys after all these years.

Her mind started to move, and she could not help thinking about a plan to implement to carry out her vengeance and get rid of Carlos. She asked Alberto, who tried in vain to dissuade her.

"Trust me, she said. I'll take care of that bastard. Just find me a weapon and when I'm done with him, we will use what we will get for ourselves in one business other than we want give us! "

Alberto was amazed by the new Griselda he discovered. This woman he had snatched from the street, to which he had made to discover its activity of smuggler to United States and who had even proved very effective in this activity, now wanted to execute the leader of a gang of thugs Puerto Rican who did not hesitate to shake down businesses under the protection of the Mafia. Was she crazy or do had she become a woman of a different kind?

He was still to wonder who she was, that Griselda went in the restaurant where the kingpin was having lunch usually. Entering this place as if she knew him, she came to him, and in a natural way, explained his project.

"You and me, we have a common enemy, she began.

-I don't see who you mean, Ma'am. I have no enemies in this neighborhood! The man did not know and did not want to take the risk of having to deal with a female cop.

-You have an enemy called Carlos Trujillo! She insisted. This man is as a pebble in your shoe. Before that it does not cause you an injury, I suggest to get rid of.

- Ah yes... and how are you doing? In stifling between your big boobs? Threw the man, looking at her up and down before turning to his bodyguards and giggle.

- I'll get rid of this man and I'll see you. At this point, you will pay me what you decide! "

She turned and left him, leaving him even no time to respond.

She returned to see Alberto and told him his interview.

"My poor Griselda, you became crazy, my word! You think you're going to liquidate Carlos and his minions will let you do without reacting?

-My love, trust me, I beg you. Find me a gun and I'm going to kill this man for what he made to me. That's eight years that I have not heard from my children. Twice, I tried to approach them in Medellin. Twice, he did send some hitters who came to threaten me to the door of my hotel room.

-You need to forget it, honey. Before the misfortune happened to us! He begged.

-This opportunity that arises is sent to me by our Madonna. How can you believe in coincidence? The world is big, so big, that we meet here, in New York, in the same neighborhood. Can what explanation you give it? "

Alberto did not insist. He knew he wouldn't have the last word and she would go at the end of his decision. Was she suicidal.

But Griselda had already designed his plan. She knew that Carlos would not withstand the urge to take her again. Not by love, just by punishment because he either wouldn't believe in coincidence. She thus enticed him, drawing him in a hotel room where he believed she would not survive him. He still believed to deal with the Griselda he knew. The low girl to whom he had given a correction. He did not, and was even far from imagine that the Griselda that had attracted him in this hotel room was a mature woman who would stop at nothing to make him pay the humiliation and the pain he had caused him. Penalty that she had borne for years.

Two days after their meeting, the body of Carlos Trujillo was found with three bullets in the body by the hotel staff.

Griselda then returned to see the boss to inform him of the death of his enemy. But this time, she stood in the company of Alberto

"So... What do you want for payment of your work? He asked taking a much more serious than air during their first interview.

- We are from Medellin, in Colombia. And we know people who can provide you with an locally manufactured flour?

- Flour? I'm no Baker?

- Colombian flour, Mister. If you are interested, we can bring you and make you taste. If you find it to your liking, then you have to pay us for it at the market price!

- I demand to see, said the man, looking Griselda, who was the only one to speak, and Alberto staring at him without blinking. Take me a small kilo, it's enough to taste! "

It was their first contact with Cosa Nostra. We were in 1968.

COSA NOSTRA

After this promising contact and several discussions between Alberto and her, they left for Colombia. They went directly in their small town of province, Medellin, sought a provider and, after many investigations, found a manufacturer of cocaine. They had to negotiate hard. We did not like a drug purchase any product, but managed to convince the manufacturer. They bought him a kilo, paying cash and promised to come back to buy more, on condition, however, he makes them a better price.

Without wasting time, they took the road by bus to Bogota, and after a dozen hours of road, went in a hotel in the area of the airport where they settled quietly. They relaxed and even made love, caught in a kind of euphoria mixed with excitement. After sleeping a few hours, they got up, went down to the restaurant of the hotel for a good breakfast and returned quietly to their rooms. It was time to get back to the business. Alberto sat down on the bed and let make Griselda, both admiring and circumspect before his energy.

She knew how and had already put on his plan to clear customs without the risk of getting caught. She took out a knife and cut the goods in two packs of five hundred grams that she then slipped into her bra.

"How did you get this idea? He asked him, amazed that she was able to think about.

-You asked me on the plane, what I used to read those magazines that you thought was ridiculous. Like this you see that my readings were not so ridiculous! " She replied without getting distracted.

She adjusted the packets of cocaine and put on the bra, positioning it so that it is less awkward as possible. Not to mention that he should not be attractive to the eyes of customs, but also of all the men she would cross between Bogotá and New York. Once this well in place, they were packing their bags and left their hotel room.

Once in the airport, she told Alberto that she wanted to buy magazines for the trip. He did not jib finally this time. In fact, she wanted to test her "apparatus" and see if the men lingered on the large breasts that made her this cocaine stuffed bra. The men that she met did not hesitate to eye up her. But as she waddled to highlight his posterior, they quickly diverted their gaze back to the level of her buttocks. His cunning seemed to work. She could therefore try to go through customs with minimal risk.

She joined Alberto, who smoked cigarette on cigarette in front of the shop, and reassured him that she was no longer confident. Set apart the attitude of her husband, nothing should make sure they are searched by customs officers.

They passed so smoothly Colombian controls, snatching smiles to police and customs officers who couldn't but to marvel at the buttocks and opulent chest of Griselda. They flew to New York and landed in the airport without obstacle. They joined their apartment in Queens, where she undressed, bringing together both packages of five hundred grams and scotch-taped them together to make only one, of a kilo that one.

"Do you think the guy is going to pay us what we're going to claim? Asked Alberto always nervous despite the fact that they have been the most difficult.

-Not only he will pay us, but he'll ask us to bring him more.

-You seem really confident, no?

-Put yourself in the place of this type. He'll have a kilo of cocaine that there lay without moving the damn bar table. What do you do best? "

Actually, it was a bargain for this guy in the borough of Queens, which was just one of many tough guys living lousy traffic beside what was the drug trafficking.

Griselda went the next day in the bar of her contact, accompanied by Alberto. It took her three days to purchase the goods and deliver the kilo of cocaine. Seeing her enter the bar where he was conducting its business, the man was more than surprised at the speed with which she had officiated and wanted more details.

"We are a group of Colombians who work in New York and, as we regularly go back with us to see our family and bring him money in order to live, we can bring back you all the goods you need, she explained without going into details.

- And that is what tells me that you don't work for the police, and you're not a fucking rat? Asked the man, worried as much efficiency and having trouble believing that she had returned to buy the goods in Colombia.

- You find that I have a head to work for the police? If this is the case, then leave it at that. If you are not interested by my merchandise, I'll sell it to someone else and is not customers lacking in New York", she chained to cut short any discussion.

She knew that this was a way to negotiate the price, but she was not prepared to negotiate. She rose from her chair and wanted to continue his package but the man immediately put his hand on cocaine to prevent Griselda resume.

"Oh, I won't make that, she addressed him glancing crucifying him on his chair. You see me maybe as a weak woman, but don't forget that it's me who put three bullets into the head of Carlos Trujillo. And kill does not scare me. So either you take my goods at the market price, or you give it to me! "

The man set to find out if she was bluffing or if she was telling the truth. He then realized the depth of his look. He looked away and looked Alberto who had, too, rose from his chair and had slipped his hand into the opening of his jacket. He had to carry a gun and, especially, seemed determined to use it despite the both bodyguards of the kingpin who were around him and, who had left their weapons.

"There is no reason to get excited, chained the kingpin, seeing that the situation skidding. But I don't have enough money on me to pay you for a kilo, he resumed.

- So send someone looking for him. Your minions must be used for something, no? You know the market price? Me too. I'm staying with you the time that we bring you the money. - She is sat back in his chair as if to nothing not was - Let me serve a double coffee, she added, showing a chair to Alberto that he comes to sit at their table, showing where all of his determination.

- Giacomo! called to the man. Use a double coffee to Madam and Mister! Pietro, come here. "

He muttered a few words in Italian in Pietro ears, one of his bodyguards, turning occasionally to Griselda to ensure that she did not understand.

"My friend will bring back me the money I pay you your kilo, he addressed Griselda.

- I thank you," she said, taking the cup of coffee that the server had brought to drink double coffee.

His hand didn't shake and the kingpin noticed his composure. "This woman has balls! " he thought.

"You told me that you could get some others? He did.

- As much as need you. But this has a cost, and we have to make it gradually, if you see what I mean.

- I see very good, Yes. "

He looked at the wall by tapping your fingers on the table his thinking time.

"This is what a kilo a week would be a good start? He proposed.

- Let's go for a kilo a week to start, she confirmed. And after a month, we can proceed two kilos...

- Done deal! "

He stopped tapping on the table and reached down to Griselda to confirm his agreement.

FIRST TRAFFICS

The following week, Alberto and Griselda left for Medellin. They bought a new kilo and returned to Bogota where they settled in the same hotel. Like the previous time, she cut it in two to slip it into her bra and adjusted it the same way. They went to the airport, returned to buy his magazines to see the reaction of the men, and be sure you can quietly pass the customs service. Again, it walked wonderfully.

So they continued thus during a few weeks before realizing that one of the officers on duty looked at her in a way that worried her. The man was no stranger to her. He had to see, and necessarily notice her because of his generous forms. Despite his fear, they passed control without trouble but, once on the plane, she explained her fears to Alberto who didn't need this to be worried.

So the next trip, they altered their route. From Medellin, they took a bus to Cartagena where they flew in a propeller plane which was a liaison with Panama-City. They then climbed on a plane of the Panam Company for New York, where they arrived safely. But it was clear that their strategy has reached its limits.

"There are two solutions, she explained to Alberto who merely follows the guidelines of his wife. Buy several pounds and hide them in other places or vary our circuits. What do you say, my dear? "

Alberto was unable to make his choice. After all, the idea came from her and she was the mastermind. But not wanting to look like a fool, he suggested her to vary the circuits.

"You're right honey, but it is also that we vary our identities. You'll find one of your contacts in New York and buy several passports. Need us to use a different identity according to the place where we will take off! "

The decision was made. But she added to this decision the fact to buy several pounds and cut them in batches to drag them elsewhere than in her bra. She made himself a ventral sheath and is slipped from the goods. And it worked perfectly, accentuating importation by varying not only departure cities but also the cities of arrival.

Over their back and forth, Griselda and Alberto began to make money. A lot of money, even. But like all things had a purpose, they grew tired of these incessant travel. If the flights were acceptable, those in car became unbearable. During one of their stay in Medellin, Griselda had an idea that Alberto called great.

They went in the neighborhood where Griselda had grown up and settled in the bar where she had stayed, not to say officiated. Accompanied by her husband, she paced the streets and noticed girls who engaged in prostitution. Some were so young that they had from the chest. They could be "mules" of choice. In the evening, in the hotel room, she explained her plan to Alberto.

"You who know people in Medellin, I want you to find a small sewing business that would manufacture us special bras.

-What is it that this idea again? He asked, completely overwhelmed by the leadership of his wife.

-We will stop taking all the risk so that others get rich on our backs. We make sure to not take any risks. I want you to make bras with compartments so that it slips the drug. On my side, I'll find girls who wear! "

It took a week for Alberto to find a small family workshop which used to work of sewing for a manufacturer of curtains. He met the head of the family, who was also the head of the company, and showed him his specimen.

"I bring the bras you and you charge me sew compartments as I've explained. There you made me ten a week. And for every bra I pay one hundred thousand pesos! "

It was a big deal that the man could refuse. This somewhat wacky story would refer to the small family business a million pesos a week. Much more than what reported them their biggest client.

"I must tell you one thing, however added Alberto. This case is strictly secret and I want to keep it. If a member of your family talking about what you make or else if he brags to earn a lot of money by sewing special bras, you not only lose the best deal you've ever made, but in addition, I will kill the person responsible for this leak. I myself do understand? "

Alberto did understand. Not only man assured him that would never happen but thanks to entrust them with this work, he kissed his hand thanking him repeatedly. It was like that that business is dealt with.

Meanwhile, Griselda had made contact with a reel, at the risk of hitting a bug because it was known that the mackerel were the major scales of the middle. But she knew the individual, and that in addition to indulge in his business of pimping, the man sometimes offered his services as hired killers. She is not unship so far. She went to meet him at home, taking the risk of being wrong, or even very badly received. To his great surprise, this was not the case. The rumor had run and the man knew who he was. This one who cared of her former husband, Carlos Trujillo, was found with three bullets in the body in a hotel of New York. How could he know this, she didn't clue but after an hour of discussion, the man revealed that he did not believe a minute that had claimed her former husband's mother.

But it was still a threat and she vowed to take care when the time comes. For now, she had to make and did not want to be distracted from what she had to put in place.

She negotiated so with the individual the supply of seven girls per week for a period of three days at the rate of a different girl every day. But unlike what the madman customers were used to ask him, she wanted girls who have the ass bigger than the chest. In however reasonable dimensions. It would pay for each girl, a million pesos a week. Charge to him to make sure with the girls sharing is as fair as possible. She knew enough this kind of individual and knew that he would not hesitate to take 90% of the money earned. She only wanted girls motivated to make the job, and the only possible motivation for these girls was that they earn more that don't all made prostitution.

The man hesitated, it wasn't in his usual to say what he had to give his daughters. But Griselda was able to find arguments to convince him that he had much more to gain by following his recommendations in the contestants.

It was as well that Griselda Blanco organized his sector to import cocaine to United States. Including the purchase of cocaine, the production of bras, the payment for the provision of the girls and the travel between Medellin and Bogota and between Bogotá and New York, had left them, Alberto and her, a few tens of thousands of dollars a week.

Beside, cocaine was not the priority of the American services to combat the drug trafficking. They put all their resources in the fight against the importation of heroin of the French traffickers had set up to move to United States. And then the cocaine was not yet a drug and the members of the medical profession had not yet declared it as truly harmful. For most of them, she was neither more nor less than a kind of hyper vitamin that consumers take to increase their sexual abilities and their fatigue resistance. For doctors, she was the image of the virtues that we gave to the leaf of coca, used for centuries by Indians.

The chain began in place. Griselda dressed her daughters with Bras adapted to their morphology and Alberto would drop them in the airport where she was taking the plane for a direct flight to New York. Once there, she found him in the toilet and gave him the bra. It worked well for several weeks to when one of the girls complained to Griselda that Alberto took advantage that he had removed her bra for fiddling her. She led his investigation and was told by other girls he was customary to the genre. She spurred an angry but affairs were foremost. And she knew that she could not make without her husband. So, as much close your eyes and make sure to let him believe that she did not know. But things get more complicated when Alberto was more content to fiddle the girls and began to have sexual relationships with several of them.

This was almost three years they were married, Alberto and her, and here is that things were, once more, badly. The men were so all the same. And if she had believed his Alberto was different from the others, she knew now that he was only one more. She then decided to change the operating mode. Waiting to find another solution and make him pay for the humiliation.

Griselda and Alberto exchanged their role. He remained in Medellin, while knowing that he would not deprive of fool around with the girls they were using, and she, moved to New York in the new apartment they had rented in the Borough of Queens. After all, since he did not deprive of send in the air with little bitches, she would take good time, also being a gigolo.

As business continued and that their sector, such a gold mine, seemed to never dry up. To such a point that she was contacted by a most important leader of the mafia. The man wanted to meet her. She accepted the appointment but was surprised that this is happening in the limousine of his interlocutor.

The man explained to her that it was his way of doing and it was the only way he found to not be listened to by the brigades of dirty cops who took particular pleasure to disrupt his business. He explained that the combat against the traffic of heroin had borne fruit, because of the increase of the condemnations and the sentences floors which had led many traffickers in prison. So that cocaine became a source of interest for members of this criminal organization, because the fight was less important. However, it was to be expected that this does not last but until the dirty cops take this drug seriously, there would be good business to make. And according to what we told him, she was the best importer of cocaine of New York. He was therefore commissioned by his organization to establish supply chains and wanted to be the best in its ranks.

She was, suddenly, the main supplier of the New York mafia, that American authorities called Crime Syndicate. It was his moment of glory and a good contrast on life.

"I didn't tell you my name, added his interlocutor.

-I didn't you it, she retorted.

-I'm John Gotti. I am the godfather of the six New York families. And it is with me, and me alone, that you will deal in this city. But there is a problem, however.

-Tell me, I might have the solution, she went on without demeaning itself.

-One of our... friends of Miami, also wants to enroll in this business. And he asked us to find someone that could provide at least four pounds a week.

-Miami? She said with a pout.

-Miami, Yes. It is a region where many Americans withdraw to spend their retirement and the aphrodisiac virtues of this medication, if I may say so, they are not, how can I...

-Don't say no more, Mister Gotti.

-Call me John.

-Don't say no more, John. Tell me only that I should go to provide the goods.

-You have to deliver the goods to the airport. A man by the name of Roberto will be waiting in a cafeteria called "Santo Christo". You will give him the goods and will receive you an envelope with the amount that we have specified.

- And how much will you give me a kilo?

-The same that we will pay you for New York.

-Give my friendships to Roberto! "

She had given his agreement. It remained only to set up a new sector between Colombia and Florida.

FIRST MILLION

The next day, Griselda flew to Bogota. The day before, at the end of the meeting, she had called Alberto and asked him to immediately stop any delivery. His first reaction was, necessarily, to understand and to worry, but she reassured him by explaining that their business development involved reorganization.

She found him in the Colombian capital, where he had made the trip to greet her. Griselda was surprised at his intention and understood her when she saw him get into a new car.

"You bought a car? He rose.

-Do you like, honey?

- But you have no driving license!

-I took a few courses and I bribed a public servant that he provides me a fake.

-A fake license? And you think that the police won't notice?

-Don't be worried, honey. It's more true than a real.

- And you think I'm going to get in your car, while you barely know how to drive?

-What's happening, you have more confidence in me? "

She no longer had confidence in him, but she could not tell him. Not yet. Especially now that their business expanded.

She resigned himself to get in his car and was driving in the new apartment Alberto had rented, clinging to the door handle during the course.

"Where are we? She asked him when he is parked.

-In our new apartment, honey! He said happy with what felt his surprise.

- And what did you make with our apartment in Medellin?

-I preferred to leave it. He was too exposed to me and, at least here, I'm only within reach of plane of you! "

Should she believe in his sincerity or was it a comedy to hide his excesses? She would know how to pull the forgery of the truth at the appropriate moment.

They entered a beautiful residence where Griselda not forbear of eyebrows by seeing the beauty of this quite new building.

"And you live here now?

-Yes, honey, I couldn't take the road between Medellin and Bogota.

- And how it goes with the girls and the goods? You deal with everything from here?

-Yes, I have everything organized like that. The girls bring me the merchandise, which I cut and then I prepare the transfer to United States. On their return, I get money, I pay the girls and I send them home.

-Why don't you let them not in Bogota until the next transfer?

-No, I don't want the girls to remain here. Like that, when they return, they deposit me the goods.

- And in Medellin, which gives them? "

That was the question that got angry. And the explanation provided by Alberto her even more angry.

"You gave to Gustavo full responsibility of girls and the purchase of the goods.

-Yes, because I know we can trust him?

- And how long do you think he's going to wait to take the thing to his account?

-He won't because I already made him sparkle then replied, knowing that she would ask him the question.

- And what did you do to sparkle? I'd like to know her? Unless you want do you it alone in business management?

-Honey, trust me. I'll explain but not before getting a hug! "

Things calmed down as well. On the pillow. It was time to move on.

Griselda was unable to accept the new organization established by Alberto. Besides answering the request of John Gotti, to double circuits between Colombia and the United States. She would therefore of the sector of New York and Alberto, of Miami. He had to find someone to manage the girls at the start of the transfer. And the choice of Gustavo turned out to be interesting but she really wanted to talk to him before entrusting him with anything. Alberto so phoned him and an interview was arranged in their apartment of Bogota.

"I learned that yesterday Alberto you had entrusted the Organization out of Medellin, she began. And my husband seems satisfied with the work you're doing, so I'll also satisfy me. But things are growing and we have to tell other things, much more important, much more profitable also necessarily, but I don't want to do without having a discussion with you, Augusto.

-Thank you for trusting me a few years ago, Griselda. I hope you have not disappointed. But know that the trusted brand that made me Alberto, warmed me the heart to a point that I would kill itself for him.

-I think we did earn too much money to this man, honey! Commented Alberto, holding a laugh that he was the only one to have.

-Not at all, Alberto. You two, the Blanco family, you did more than just make money. You gave me a social position. Much better than if I had continued to protect girls on the sidewalk. And this, I'll never forget. So be certain that I will do everything I can not to disappoint you! "

It was a form of thanks, which pleased Griselda, surprise by this form of allegiance. The bastard who put girls on the sidewalk without scruples that they bring him money, showed another angle. Gustavo Ramirez was their first official employee.

Griselda and Alberto, they, in turn, turned their attention to receive the "mules" who delivered cocaine to New York and Miami. The process was simple: after having passed the customs controls, the girl went to the airport bathroom where she found either Griselda, when she landed in New York, Alberto when she landed in

Miami. Two leaders exchanged them the bra where cocaine with another containing dollars that they had to rely on their return that awaited them in Bogota.

Half of the money was then distributed between the provider of cocaine in Medellin, the purchase of special bras, the commission of setters, and various fees. The other half was Gustavo.

Traffic worked this way for months. Customs officials did nothing because women used several passports and multiple identities to avoid detection. Business walked so that in 1972, Mr. and Ms. Bravo won their first million dollars.

A HIGH-TECH INDUSTRY

The chains Bogota-New York and Bogota-Miami found themselves quickly enough to supply the demand of the North American market. They needed to increase routing circuits. But regular flights between the capital of Colombia and the two American cities were insufficient. Even by placing several mules in a same plane, it took a dozen daily flights to provide customers from the Bravo network, name of Griselda and Alberto.

Both spouses decided to organize a meeting in Bogota with their relay, Gustavo Ramirez. He should think about a solution to provide the ten pounds daily requested by John Gotti, Godfather of the New York Mafia families and the other five pounds required by the new Godfather of Miami, Santo Traficcante Junior. In fact, there is a solution. Since he was not enough of aircraft to the departure of Bogota, it was enough to set up another channel and go to another city. But this meant to give it to someone else.

Gustavo spoke to them from a family of horse breeders, resident in Medellin and accustomed to travel their horses to provide their foreign customers. So they knew how to practice to get the borders at the goods. Even though it was quite different. As for his case, Griselda asked to meet them. A date was made.

It did well for a long time that Griselda had not returned to Medellin. And the visual shock it surprised her. It was the city where she had grown up and should not be so surprised. However, this changed her in his neighborhood of Queens where homes, yet modest, were still less miserable. But she couldn't help but have a twinge seeing those poorly dressed children, some barefoot, playing in the street. She thought of her son, who had to grow well since she had not seen them, and unfortunately, she couldn't afford to go see because his ex mother-in-law did the rumor that she had killed her son, Carlos. She would take care of that when the time comes, she said to herself again, repeating these words whenever she remembered her boys. But she was still taken penalty, especially when they saw these young girls who patrolled the sidewalks to sell their charms. "Thus is the world" she said picking up her spirits to only focus on what had brought her back in this city.

They surrendered in the vicinity of Medellin and arrived in a farm where they caught sight of the land on which frolicked horses. It was the domain of the Ochoa family. One area where they practiced the breeding and training of racehorses or parade.

Gustavo presented them to Jorge, the father and chief of the clan. They settled in a patio where a servant brought them drinks.

"Senor Ochoa, began Gustavo, I present to you Griselda and Alberto Bravo, the both people I told you about and who would like to use your skills in the logistics field to export goods to United States.

-To United States, said Jorge Ochoa. In what city?

-Miami! Said Griselda tit for tat.

- And what kind of merchandise? He asked of an air which left no doubt about his suspicion.

-A product which the Andean peasants grow and which love the gringos! "

Discussion ensued and ended two hours later with an agreement for the amount paid per delivery. Alberto however had to organize the supply of the goods to their field where Jorge Ochoa would organize the transfer to Miami where Alberto and Griselda would receive the merchandise. The agreement fell on hundred pounds a week to be delivered in five times. What amounted to twenty pounds per delivery.

But before leaving, she asked an interview one-on-one to Jorge Ochoa, surprising her husband and his associate, both exhausted and anxious to be away from this discussion.

"Señor Jorge, you have three sons? She said.

-Yes Griselda. Three boys whom I thrilled me to see grow with each passing day.

-I have three boys, too!

-You have three sons?

-Si Señor. Dixon, Uber and Osvaldo. They are here in Medellin. Their father, Carlos Trujillo, deprived them to me before threw me in the street. I'm twenty years old and I have never seen them since.

-I heard a story in this regard...

-I went to live in New York and God, or rather the Virgin Mary who knows what a mother feels, has liked us ourselves in the same neighborhood, he and I. Yet, the world is big, Señor Jorge. But it took him to come live a few blocks from where I lived. How should I take this, in your opinion, if it wasn't a desire to humiliate me further.

-This is strange indeed, he said, wary.

84

-So I gave her an appointment in a cheap hotel and I put three bullets in the body. Two in the heart and once in the head for those police officers believe a crime carried out by a hired killer.

-Were you, Griselda, I would have done the same thing! He approved.

-Their grandmother told my son that I had killed their father, and they do not seek to try to see again me. I'll be thirty next year and it will be ten years I am without news of my children who have been growing well since. I don't even know if I know them by crossing them in the street.

- And what would you have me do, Griselda?

-My eldest is certainly working age. Maybe even others. You have a beautiful farm, Señor Jorge. Maybe you have work for them...

-I will certainly find something to give them to, Griselda. And I will give them even a good salary. Even though I think you would not like to they give a portion to their grandmother.

-Not at all, on the contrary. I have nothing against this woman. And I bless her even of taking care of my son.

-I already use your eldest son, Griselda. If this goes well, I'll take his younger brother then the last, if everything goes better in the world. I will give them a good salary in return for the money that you will allow me to win with the organization of transfers of your goods.

-I will be eternally grateful, Señor Jorge. "

She rose from her chair and took Jorge Ochoa in his arms, under the inquiring eye of Alberto and Gustavo.

When she joined them, she passed before them without mark stop and returned to the car, eyes filled with tears. Alberto asked her the reasons for her tears and she said simply that she had requested a service to their new partner which had accepted it thanking her for this vote of confidence and this had touched her.

The new network was quickly set up and it worked perfectly the first time. The second and the following passed well. But after a few months, Alberto complained to Griselda to be nailed in Miami, this old town where he could not stand the atmosphere or climate. She pretended to believe but knew the real reason of his annoyance.

"Just give me a few days to arrange and I'll replace you in Florida."

If Alberto could not stand the climate of Florida, Griselda, her, couldn't the cold of New York. She would settle in Miami where she would find a Latin atmosphere, and would take her husband back to Bogota where he could fool around with which he would, provided that he continues to deliver the goods to New York City.

A week later, Griselda landed on the Miami Airport, accompanied by a certain Ramon. She introduced him to Alberto and explained him was his best reseller, as she was, of course, not merely to provide exclusively the mafia and had set up a network of resale in the latino neighborhood where consumers were not lacking.

Alberto is annoyed as he ever did. He was dying to administer a beating to his wife but the presence of the man who was with him, forced him to hold his arm. After all, he got what he wanted and once in Bogota, he could make what he wanted. Alberto returned in Colombia and organized the delivery of the goods, via Florida because New York knew of turnovers.

The American Government, to the instigation of the president Richard Nixon, had declared total war against drug trafficking which, according to the press, was more deaths by overdose as the Viet Nam war. A large media campaign was launched in 1972 to end what the authorities called the "French Connection", after the release of a film that explained the Organization of traffic via France and the involvement of a mafia of Corsican origin. The increased sentencing floors rang the death knell for this traffic and many mafiosi wanted to mingle the traffic of other white powder, cocaine.

Griselda negotiated with John Gotti, but before the pressure and the threats, criminal as police, she had to give up and concede to the Mafia organization for resale in any of the neighborhoods of New York. In return, she obtained a monopoly on delivery to the cities that ruled Cosa Nostra.

She returned to Bogota, explained what she considered a good agreement, and asked Alberto to organize other routes because demand continued to increase. Together, they returned to Medellin and met Jorge Ochoa and Gustavo Ramirez. This latter explained to them that they were not able to manage as many goods and presented a small local thug who tampered high-tech goods, especially TVs, between Colombia and Bolivia. Griselda knew view and when he greeted her, she could not help him to report.

"I knew a Pablo Escobar Gaviria in my youth, she said. You're not?

-It's me, Ms. Bravo, he confirmed.

-Call me Griselda. Here, everyone is called by his first name.

-It's me, Griselda, he resumed.

-I was told that you were selling goods in Bolivia? But what Bolivians can buy you?

-I sell washing machines laundry, TVs, and whatever they ask me, Griselda. And I organize these trades with my cousin Gonzalo.

- And how do you pay? With their currency of monkey?

-They pay us with a coca paste that we resell to Colombian chemists. And I must say it's a good business. "

She turned to Jorge Ochoa and Gustavo Ramirez.

"It is he who gives you the raw, right? She asked them.

-It is quite this, Griselda, said Gustavo Ramirez. Us, we turn this dough in powder and we resell it to you. But today, our production capacity is limited and we need so increase the number of manufacturers. As we are already working with Pablo, we believe he could enter our trade and become partner. "

She turned again to Pablo Escobar Gaviria and looked at him in eyes several seconds without lowering the gaze. He also did not give the eyes.

"Our business is growing and we need to increase our production capacity. But to produce, we need goods. A lot of goods. Then, Pablo Escobar Gaviria, is welcome in our organization. But he is going to need that we specify the details of our organization, the responsibilities of each and, above all, the amount of which is up to each.

-Be sure, Griselda, that I shall dedicate myself bodies and souls to your organization. "

We were in 1973. Their association was the preamble to what would become in the late 1980s, the Medellin Cartel.

They returned the next day after spending the night in the hacienda of the Ochoa family. Griselda looked at two young boys work as farm boys. It was his two sons, Dixon and Uber. She could not help being taken of emotion. They were beautiful and big, as was their bastard of father. She was dying to talk to them, to take them in his arms, but she held him back, fearing that they don't grow back. He should make the time and wait for them to forget bad things that their grandmother had to put them in the head.

Griselda and Alberto returned to Bogota. They finalized the new threads, and then she went on a flight to New York. On the plane where she was, a dozen mules made, they also, the trip. Enough to provide a few days at the New York mafiosi.

Alberto, he, undertook to implement the new organization. He developed the new network and the money began to fill their coffers until it becomes problematic.

A solution was needed to whiten, said specialists. Bankers were contacted so that they take care to place millions of dollars in business that needed to be profitable. It wasn't question to squander anything, even if the zeros were piling up.

Finally alone, Alberto began to take some liberties, in addition to those that he was already engaged in pleasures of the flesh with the mules he employed. He began snorting this cocaine, which he sold in large quantities. After all, since it was predicted it aphrodisiac, as not to miss. But that is not enough. Nor the mules he thanked in the worst way, sometimes abusing of them. He bought a luxury mansion on the heights of Bogota.

"To work more peacefully without being under the threat of intervention of the police and enjoy the freshness of the forest ", he told to Griselda who believed nothing of what he said.

Especially since next to the hacienda, he built a relaxing space for door-guns watching over him can be entertained without having to leave the area. In this space, he opened a bar, a restaurant and a nightclub that he called the Bora Bora Club. For what leave no doubt about what was happening. Because the girls were not lacking. And the most beautiful and the most appetizing were, necessarily, reserved for the boss.

Meanwhile, the business continued under the benevolence of Griselda and his associates who were running the machine. And it worked perfectly, although Alberto got further and further, entrusting responsibilities to his straw men and devoted more to split his time between the party, with a consumption of alcohol and drugs, and the girls who did not empty any more his bed. Everything was going so well, that a kind of routine moved, especially because business turned without barriers and because they grew at an incredible speed. And in criminal activities, there was nothing worse that the routine because it meant lower our guard and take risks.

We were in 1975.

A music began to invade the clubs and nightclubs. As was a dance music, was called Disco. And its well-known choruses became a fashion phenomenon and filled a little more places where you could dance and where, those who danced through the night, began to consume a product more popular, and that is lent some virtues, cocaine.

This white powder was now mass consumed and replaced the alcohol vapors for lovers of excesses of all kinds. Those who were selling it to shoeing to meet the demand. And the sales began to gain huge amounts of money for those who did trade because every month, it was more than a ton which entered the North American territory.

Alberto, who was not left to follow the fashions of this time, decided to make a big delivery to New York. But for this, he needed the agreement of those who represented the authority in their network, his wife Griselda. So he asked her to come and spend a few days in Bogota to explain his plan.

She made the trip and discovered the home that her husband had been build on the hills in North of Bogota and the buildings he built around. The Bora Bora Club. She could have a sermon, but checked himself. First, because her relationship with her husband had become so remote that they shared more than the interests of their business, and then, because she had come for this reason. In fact, when Alberto asked her to settle in her room, she asked him where the guest room. It does not contradict the most for not that she opposes the plan that he had designed and installed her in the biggest rooms of guests from his hacienda.

Barely his affairs were put, Griselda asked Alberto to explain the reasons for his request.

"Honey, he began, have you heard of what the gringos getting ready for July 4, 1976?

-I heard nothing except that they will celebrate their national day every year, she replied.

-Yes, but this time, they prepare something of monumental. You know the gringos and their taste for everything related to their country?

-Explain what you want to make and avoid beating around the bush, she cut him off.

-They plan to organize a parade of ships in the bay of New York. And our Government, you know as our politicians like to lick the boots of those sons of bitches of gringos, offered to sail a boat that we use, we, on 12 October to celebrate the feast of the discovery of America by Christopher Colomb.

- And so?

- And so as this boat must start from Cartagena to New York, I figured we could load it goods. What do you say?

- And how do you plan to make? She asked, interested by the idea.

-I made contact with the captain of this ship, and I offered him a million dollars to deliver the goods.

-$ 1 million? But do you know how much it takes to deliver kilos for get back this money?

-Yes dear, I know. We will charge five hundred kilos of goods on this boat. What do you say?

-Five hundred pounds? In just one delivery? But you fell on your head or what? Since when we deliver as many goods in one drop? Can you imagine what would happen if the customs fell on?

-I have everything, my dear. Everything happen as planned.

-I do not agree. It's too risky.

-Not at all, dear. And to be sure those things will turn right, I will make the trip with the boat. And my bodyguards will accompany me.

- And me, in all of this?

-You, darling, you wait us in New York where you take care of the unloading and you'll find a place to store the goods. That's why I brought you here my dear.

-Five hundred pounds! You are crazy, Alberto! "

Finally, it was 150 pounds which were loaded on the boat. Not because the risk was too great but because Griselda had convinced his suppliers to settle for not delivering more goods to Alberto. She found her interesting the plan, of course, but she didn't trust this commander, which was before any official, and which could, at any time, sell the wick to the Colombian authorities and, worst of all, American.

On 25 June, the Colombian boat, "Tall Ship Gloria", called so to pay tribute to the carrack Santa Maria, flagship of Christopher Colomb, when he began his journey to the West to find the route to India, entered the Bay of New York and headed the Hudson River where the pier where the boat was moored. But hardly the moorings were thrown, cars appeared, all sirens blaring. Alberto understood what was to follow. Accompanied by his bodyguards, they jumped on the platform and began to run toward the sheds where they hoped to be able to hide. After several minutes of track race and implausible panic because shots that derived from part and other, the DEA agents came at the end of the fugitives.

The eight door-guns that accompanied Alberto were all arrested. Several of them were wounded by the shots fired by agents of the DEA. Alberto, him, had better luck. He find Griselda and his hands awaiting them in vans to load the goods. This team there managed to leave the port to the nose and beard of the multitude of officers committed to intervention. They took refuge in the New York latino neighborhood where they felt sufficiently safe. But not for long as it was clear that someone had denounced them.

And those who has made was no doubt.

"I told you that I had no confidence in this Commander, Griselda criticized to Alberto. Not only the goods are lost but it is going to need that we quickly leave from here! "

Alberto was silent because he knew she was right. Besides, time was not for the discussion. He had to clear this country before the DEA agents don't put hands on them.

"You're going to go back to Bogota, she ordered without giving him the choice. You're going to take care of our business and you'll let me take care of that son of a bitch who sold us. And I also have to reorganize my network until the DEA agents go back up the circuit. I'll meet you when I have organized all this! "

Alberto listened and continued to be silent. He knew that he had no interest to say anything, because of the circumstances and because the 'big one' he hoped to male to grow in importance in the eyes of their associates had gone wrong. He already saw himself in the role of chief with the success of the operation that he had got the idea and he had organized only. But now that things had gone wrong, he had interest to make carpet and just look after shipping the goods from Bogotá. As he had to quickly find a way to deliver content that the boat contained to meet the demands of their customers.

Once in Bogota, he took over the classical chain with mules but added them a belt containing two kilos of cocaine. After all since customs officers noticed anything about bras, there no reason that they suspect that strong breasts and ass as round, women belly. He therefore loaded his mules to three pounds of powder and filled the planes with a dozen girls on each trip.

In New York, Griselda, who was hiding for not being arrested by narcotics officers, continued to receive the goods. She had just reorganized the sector of reception and had recruited other men to hand, in case those who worked for her would be monitored by the DEA.

But she couldn't bring herself to accept the idea that someone had denounced them. The commander knew the risks he was running by agreeing to move the merchandise, it's drugs anyway, but it was inconceivable that he agreed to denounce them, knowing what awaited him on his return to Colombia. So, who would denounce them?

She turned over and over a thousand and a thousand times the issue. What was the most surprising, it was his business to her continued and that she noticed no oversight on the part of the agents of the DEA. An investigation was underway, but she had to fear no direct threat. This continued for several months until one day, a squad of DEA agents stop several of his henchmen and back the chain to a warehouse where she stored the goods. By chance, they seized only eight kilos of cocaine. But the worm was in the fruit and the tree might be contaminated.

Some of its dealers began to speak for the last measure put in place by the American Government: the protection of informants. Therefore, nothing prevented the scales swing. And when she began to investigate to find out how the DEA had the information, she had to go to a no-brainer: If someone had denounced them, was that Alberto was under the supervision of the members of the Colombian police, who informed the DEA agents. They had then to follow the mules goes from Bogota to traced back to her.

An arrest warrant was even launched against her after that 30 of its dealers have been arrested and that narcotics officers have seized 100 kilograms of goods. There was an emergency because the penalty was 15 years in prison. She spurred an angry and was threaten with death those who spoke, she had only one thing to make: leave the American territory and return to Colombia where she could rebound. She went to the bus station and took a bus to Miami. It was the safest way to leave town without risking to be apprehend.

There, after many hours on the road to moping and curse those who had put an end to his juicy case, she said that the only way to regain this trade was to get rid of those who had contributed to end. She was tired of having to bear the problems caused by others. To begin with her husband.

Once in Miami, Griselda returns to see his contact, Alberto, and informed him of the bad turn of events in New York. He reassured her and told her that in Florida, she would be safe. But she is not heeded and said she preferred to return to Colombia where she would feel much more safe. Even more, she had to reorganize the sector as a result of the DEA agents had updated the delivery by the mules. Given that this sector had been discovered, more no delivery would be made by this way. If he guaranteed her that Miami was safe at this point, so all deliveries would arrive in this city. Support to him to make sure to deliver the goods in the rest of the country.

Alberto could not but rejoice about what he had learned. Griselda would now deal with exports and would be responsible for the distribution on North American soil. He had to step up and, on condition however that things go well, he would certainly win millions of dollars. Fortune had smiled to him.

Meanwhile, Griselda asked him to find a plane back to Bogota. She held not to make the trip by boat and knew that a warrant of arrest in his effigy was circulating in the customs services. She wouldn't take the risk to go to the airport.

Griselda so flew into a comfortable jet in the direction of Bogota. It was the first time that she was getting into this type of device and appreciated the luxury. Even though she knew she was his return trip to the country, forced and obliged. She didn't even know if she would ever return to United States and said that this trip could be the last because she had decided to take a drastic action.

It was a feminine way to treat an itch that nothing calmed. Since this itch could be soothed that scratching her, then simply scratch, again and again, until the blood appears, even hurt.

And Griselda had decided to get hurt. Very hurt.

A NEW DIRECTION

In this day of May 1977, the air traffic of the airport Eldorado-Bogota was suspended to allow a small private plane arriving from Miami to land. The person who was on board to be a head of State or something of the sort for the airport director decides to disrupt air traffic.

The Falcon, a French-made jet, landed on the runway and headed a shed well out of sight. Once inside, the driver parked the aircraft and cut the reactors. When the door opened, six men went down the device while three big black Cadillac, waiting patiently for the arrival, approached. The men organized a string and passed the impressive number of suitcases. It was true that Griselda had redone her wardrobe when she found herself stuck in Miami. She had to leave everything in New York to not load by taking the bus but she still wasn't coming back to the country with little business because she didn't know how long she would have to stay there before returning to United State.

The six men sided suitcases into the coffers of the first two vehicles and returned to the foot of the stairs to greet the person coming down and make him a sort of hedge of honor. So much for protection to honor him. A little woman went down the plane by taking his time, holding back a smile when he saw those men who stood there with attention. Before descending, she took the time to change to not look as one of those mules that employed her. She was dressed with a tailor and a red cloche hat Yves Saint Laurent and his eyes were hidden by sunglasses of French brand, too. She had completed her look with a handbag pink Lancel, another French brand, which was all the rage in United States. She climbed in the second car, after that the driver had opened the door, taking care to not offend his tailor. The six men went up them, in two other vehicles which began without delay.

The convoy came out of the shed and walked toward the exit, at the end of the departure hall at brisk pace. Not because there was urgency but because it was as drivers were driving. In most of these American cars to boxes automatic were real bombs. It was enough to press the accelerator so that they leave at full speed. The motorcade left the airport and reached to the hills to the northeast of the city. It was here that Alberto Bravo had built his hacienda. "To enjoy the freshness of nature," he said. "You're going to see what I do with your coolness, son of a bitch," she murmured in whisper for that does not hear the driver.

Alberto had wanted to a warm reception to his wife for his return to the country. He knew that she it was close to New York, as he had decided to make her forget this disappointment. He had sent his three most beautiful cars. To complete this home, he had a small party where she could forget her misfortunes and appreciate the return to Colombia.

But Griselda had not come to party. Far from it. That's almost three years she lived the bulk of the year in United States and that she no longer shared the bed with Alberto. More nothing not bound them, except for their business. And they had done wrong to end because of the recklessness of her husband she put on the account of his frivolity. She had been pleased when she began dating the man who would become her second husband. But with time, their relationship was more fragile and since Alberto took womanizing habits, so put an end to their matrimonial relationship.

Officially, his trip to Colombia was aimed to reorganize their chains. But another intention had forced her to return, other than having to leave the American territory. And that was only what had convinced her to take the path of return of this country.

After two interminable hours of road, the convoy arrived in the hacienda of Alberto and discovered the Bora Bora Club, the place where he organized lavish parties by inviting all the girls who wanted to win his esteem. Can't be in his bed. Besides, on perceiving the damsels who twittered with the guards, she understood how the Colombian police had managed to spot the activity of Alberto Bravo funny and could thus inform American authorities who had put an end to his lucrative business.

Griselda now knew who was responsible for what was happened. She already suspected, but arriving here, she was more than convinced. She opened her Lancel bag and slipped the hand to caress the gun she had for years and that he had repeatedly brought luck. After using it to liquidate Carlos Trujillo, she would use to end Alberto Bravo. Two causes for the same effect.

But the man held for his safety. For this, he was surrounded by a swarm of bodyguards. These men looked all out of the same mold. Between thirty and forty years, the look made arrogant by the power that granted them the weapons they were carrying to the size. It was enough to little knowledge to see they weren't things that primary, devoid of intelligence, apart from lacking beasts of conscience that made them kill anyone without any remorse.

Griselda knew that his only chance would be the element of surprise which would of course those door-guns, busier fiddling with girls that were used as mules. Since the industry had to be reorganized, they were there to look after taking good time with big arms.

When the cars stood in front of the house, Alberto went out in the parking lot to accommodate his wife as he had planned. The cars stopped at the foot of the staircase leading to the house. Griselda went down and removed his sunglasses to see this man she hated, now, more than anything after having loved him so much better. The happiness she had known to him eventually make him forget the rage that lived it to meet them. But with time and the excesses of her husband, hatred had finished replacing all.

Griselda remained near to the limo and made him sign to approach in the hope that he would solve. Alberto, who had no idea of what his wife had reserved, complied, smiling and spreading the arms to better serve his happiness to see her again. Four bodyguards, who never left alone, had not fitted. She sketched a supported smile and tried, as well as to hide his annoyance.

"I learned that you had trouble in New York, he began.

-Yes, it took me to leave but not without getting money that I put aside, thankfully. In fact, I brought it! " Threw to force him to approach.

Alberto, won by the desire to see what she was talking about, approached a little more.

"And there are many? He ventured to ask.

- Yes, there's got to be a few million. And half is for you," she added to bait him.

Alberto wanted at all costs to see that closely. So he did the few steps which still separated him from the car.

"But more than that, I brought a personal gift that you don't forget about me ever!" She threw again.

Griselda opened of a dry gesture her handbag, slid his hand there and took out her revolver. Neither Alberto nor the bodyguards, who didn't expect at all to it, had no time to react. She opened fire on her husband and emptied the six bullets that contained the charger to make sure not missed. The six men who were with her came out, in turn, their weapons and took care four body guards to ensure that they have a reaction that could be dramatic. A real worthy of Ok Corral backfiring began. The door-guns of Alberto fell one after the others. But two of the men of Griselda also were shot. Griselda, she was hit on the belly. He had to transport her to the hospital and get out in speed until the other men come running and liquidate them all. Quickly and unceremoniously, they put her in the limo and the procession began with a bang.

The drivers tried to escape. But they had not had time. And that was with a gun to the head led by keeping the same pace to go. In fact, it was better for them go away also because the men, who came in brandishing weapons of war, would shoot in the heap without worrying about the fate of the drivers.

"Take me to the Margotal clinic, muttered Griselda, bad. The director is a friend. "

On the path that took her, she thought about the consequences of her act. She knew that her former husband's family did not react. Alberto had involved some of his members to their traffic and it was clear that she would not accept the murder without wanting to shut her down. She had better go ahead and settle on behalf of all those involved, from near or far, to their business. It was the sine qua none to stay alive. And in her case, she was expecting what they do suffer there is worse.

"As soon as I arrive in the clinic, I have to call my associates of Medellin and pray them to make what she had asked them before leaving Miami." She said to herself in an attempt to stay awake.

She knew she could trust them. Even if in business the confidence was a thing the outcome of which we never knew. Until it turns to his advantage, he had to keep her alive. And saying this, she could not help thinking about his boys watching the road that passed through the colorful windows of the limousine.

Once in the clinic, his men began the emergency service on the alert. Service nurses had also already reacted when he saw the three Cadillac enter at high speed in the parking lot where many pebble of the ground had been planned around when the tires had creaked. Griselda was placed on a stretcher and quickly taken to the operating room. The doctor who examined her, noticed the hole shot in the abdomen. Absolutely had to get the bullet out until things get rough. But attention to the result of the operation, slipped one of the bodyguards to the doctor who would perform the surgery.

Fortunately, the injury was slight and did not ask major surgery. All only lasted about ten minutes. Griselda was then taken in a single room on the top floor of the clinic for more security. The four bodyguards moved in front of the door of the room, making the foot of crane in the hallway. They were the ones who had Griselda Blanco's life in hands.

The drivers had been dismissed after being warned that if they indicated the place where they were deposited Griselda, they would be killed, just like their women and their children, for those who were, but also the others members of their family. And to watch their backs, he had been told in gratitude, they would be used by the owner to conditions they have ever had with Alberto Bravo.

Thirty minutes after his operation, Griselda woke up. She looked around her and called. His loyal lieutenant entered immediately. She was far out and was already thinking about what was to follow.

"You're going to call our friends in Medellin and ask them two things. First, make what I told them when I called them to Miami. And second, tell Jorge Ochoa make away my children because I'm afraid that the Alberto family gets to them if they can't find me"

The man complied in the second when she turned her head to look out. She had not been on a hospital bed since his birth. It was years ago. And turning in his bed, the pain tore a grimace. She had been hot this time.

But who was? She thought back to her life, to the trials of his existence because something inside she demanded to know why. At the result of his actions on those who crossed his way, in that it resulted in the world that surrounded him, insisted the voice inside of her to ask why for the men that she had loved were condemned to die from his hand. She had become indifferent to the feelings she had experienced for them? Why was her life made of adversity, of fighting to lead? Was she designed to hurt? Could she not everything just to love and be loved, like everything else? Why God called him his trials? Should she still pay for what Eve had done? And how women should be punished for serving this damnation?

She drove her thoughts because she refused to leave her feminine side take over and decrease his merits. It was probably the effect of the anesthetic that had brought him his thoughts, said woke up an hour later. She had taken a risk. A big risk even but now, it was she who was the real leader of the entire network. The only one to order without having to share the gains with a husband who took a good time while she was doing all the work or decisions. She was going to be able to reorganize everything in its way, with her friends in Medellin, and when everything would be in place, she would return to Miami.

MIAMI VICE

Griselda had to stay a week in the clinic. At the same time to recover and to stay away the time that her friends have been the household. Alberto Bravo's family was decimated by his partners, Gustavo Ramirez, who now called himself the Mariachi to give itself a genre, the Ochoa family, whose sons had taken the notes of his father Jorge and cousins Escobar Gaviria, Pablo and Gonzalo.

But it had a price. Not only to pay the Sicarios who executed the contracts, and that some were killed in their turn, but also to compensate those who in had taken. Because during this time, the deliveries of goods were stopped. And the goods accumulated in warehouses. But Griselda not worried so far. Because she knew that any shortage had direct consequence to raise the price. And all lost money would be offset by the gain would give the price increase by the gram, which would affect, necessarily, this one per kilo.

Griselda had decided to eliminate her husband to make her pay for his excesses and the risks that he had made him run by building this brothel that had attracted the attention of the police on him and, of course, on his activities which allowed him to spread his extravagant wealth. But not only. Although she had to quickly leave the American territory, she had managed to take with her the accumulated money and who was in the suitcases stored in the coffers of two Cadillac. This was over three million dollars. So she decided to only keep only a third and give the other two million to her associates to thank them for having made the wanted work.

After be recovered, Griselda left the Margotal clinic and left Bogota behind her. She returned to Medellin to meet with her partners and set up a new organization. Because during the days she spent in her room, she had resumed contact with clients who had worried about her absence and who no longer knew how to satisfy the demand of their customers. She had reassured them by saying that his troubles in New York had forced her to leave United States but not the business. In fact, she was already working to reorganize the transfers of goods and told them that she would soon be there to oversee the deliveries. But what she didn't tell them, it was how she saw the future.

She spent a week in Medellin and set up her new organization. Now, the deliveries will be made in Miami, where his contact Alberto kept a close watch until she can return to it. But the lines were going to be different. No more question to pass the goods with mules. Now, the deliveries would be made by boat and even by plane. It was enough to find drivers that could take care of the delivery. The procedure would be the following: it took over several ships, which would stopover to Haiti to refuel fuel, where military officials of the dictator in place would welcome them, then the ships would take the direction of the coast of Florida. For what was in aircraft deliveries, aircraft should drop bundles of goods off the coast of Florida where accomplices would recover them by using small boats equipped with big engines.

Things started well in place. The partners of Medellin took charge to deliver the goods in Florida and Griselda and his right-hand man, Alberto, would sell. Two-thirds were delivered to New York, where John Gotti undertook to allocate it among the other Boss of Cosa Nostra, and the other party was sold by the men of the network of Griselda. Everything went perfectly and the million mounted. To the extent that it now took care to launder this money to the more discreet ways.

This was rather easy. Especially since the new president of United States, Ronald Reagan, and the British Prime Minister, Margaret Thatcher, had decreed the liberalization of the movement of capital. This decision was intended to attract their countries capitalists of the world.

The president of Unites States had decided to engage in a tug of war with the Soviet Union, which had invaded its neighbor, Afghanistan, and had increased the military budget as this had not happened since the Viet Nam war. If you add the tax reductions, the American State was at the edge of apoplexy, not to say the bankruptcy. He needed money to compensate for it. And the best way for a State to get money without borrowing it was to issue Treasury bonds. The machine print these coupons worked so continuously. And all buyers were welcome, whatever they may be.

The other way was to invest in the stock market. Wall Street had been brought to heel by Franklin Roosevelt after the crash of 1929 when the Black Thursday had caused the collapse of the stock market. But it was no longer there. Then the big bankers of Manhattan took advantage of the arrival to power of Ronald Reagan, who wanted less State in the economy, to demand an end to regulations from the New Deal, brake for economic development for them. Also, they put the threat of tax havens, which attracted many American capital.

In response, president Reagan authorized the creation of Bank zones, the International Banking Facilities, where American Bankers could lend money to foreign residents, while being exempt from various taxes. The internal market was, therefore, deregulated and several American States, Texas, Florida, and Nevada in mind, developed mechanisms to attract money from abroad.

Taking advantage of what American authorities allowed, Griselda bought a penthouse on the top floor of a building. This apartment was immediately pleased her because the windows opened on Biscayne Bay. And with millions she earned, she might even have to buy the whole building. His business was so juicy that at forty, she earned up to 80 million dollars a month. She could splurge, but she feared to soften and expose herself as did her former husband, Alberto Bravo.

Another way to launder dirty money was to go through the banks of the former possessions of the British Empire, transformed into havens for the size of their economy. "Rule Britannia" said these experts who were recovering billions of dollars that they kept in the City of London using the flexibility of the English State services.

Tax havens exist to attract capital by allowing their owners to prosper by circumventing the laws and regulations of their country of origin, through a policy of secrecy, dating back to 1862. In this jurisdiction of secrecy, cash would arrive by private jet and, sometimes, a police escort accompanied even the armored truck that picked up the trunks of bills to deposit in the banks.

In fact, the history of tax havens showed a convergence between British officials and the underworld. The image of Bahamas, which the English dealers supplied weapons to the slave States of the South of United States during the American civil war. Meyer Lanski, the right arm of the famous Lucky Luciano, offered a bribe of $ 1.8 million to the Governor of Bahamas to make him pass legislation making the violation of banking secrecy a criminal offence. Despite the warnings from officials of the IRS and the British Treasury, London gave its green light.

Tax havens were divided into four groups. The first consisted of those located in Europe. The second was centered in the City of London, bringing together the former British colonies around the world. The third was under the sphere of influence of United States. And the fourth consisted of a few countries such as Somalia and Uruguay, but whose unreliability drew few candidates.

Because tax havens were not only banks to launder dirty money around the world. They were also networks of influence at the service of the States that would let them conduct this policy of secrecy. Starting with United States, masters of the world of finance, and Britain which supported the fourteen colonial entities having denied independence, such as Bermuda, the British Virgin Islands, Cayman Islands, Turcques and Caicos Islands or even Gibraltar, and which had a financial link with the City of London through the Bank of England.

The Bank of England was founded in 1694 in the form of a rich London bankers club. It was nationalized in 1946 to allow the British Government to help the country to recover destruction of World War II. But even under the thumb of the State, the Governor of the Bank was not appointed by the Government and was recruited from among the best managers of the financial companies in the City. She continued to operate under the cover of secrecy.

To achieve its purposes, the Bank of England played a central role in the creation of Euromarket, by developing new financial mechanisms. These mechanisms enabled the liberalization of the world economy by being the main source of capital in the world. In 1980, Euromarket represented a value of $ 500 billion. Seven years later, the value was 2600 billion.

Griselda controlled the traffic of cocaine between Colombia and Miami which demand kept growing. So much so that she was now a ton and a half of this merchandise each month. A ton and a half which she resold a third in his network and which brought her near to $ 3 million each day calendar. Her skills were such that they allowed her to multiply the number of friends in Cosa Nostra. His representative in Miami, Santo Traficcante Junior, was even part of her respondents.

But now that the Cuban Government, in response to a request of the American Government, freed many political prisoners. He took the opportunity to get rid of common law prisoners and sent to United States via Florida, what the country had as thugs.

These men, arrived in conquered land, began to indulge in all of the abuses. And there was no more juicy than the sale of cocaine. Many Cubans got so in this trade and began to compete with dealers Colombian and Puerto

Rican. He had to show these "Chicanos" which was the real master.

She was sending a specialist of the genre: Jorge Ayala, nicknamed Riverito.

The man was a weapons expert. Former soldier of elite of the Colombian army that had fought revolutionaries, he knew to show all his talents to the service of his country. But this one had been ungrateful with him denying that there are worse for a man who wanted a career in army at the risk of his life: the right to move up the ranks. Because Jorge Ayala put too much zeal to accomplish the missions we confided and left too many dead bodies behind him. Sometimes even simple peasants who had been unlucky enough to live in a war zone. Jorge Ayala, convinced that they were bringing aid to those he was fighting, punish them all, making even to dig the mass graves to men to bury their women and their children. This was strongly displeased the officers who had forced him to resign, claiming he dirty the military uniform. Necessarily, because them simply to make war behind clean and air-conditioned offices.

So Jorge Ayala was put at the service of those who did not hesitate to use violence to defy the authorities. He thus obtained his revenge by taking the ranks while adjusting the account to officers, even if they were police officers. Didn't matter him, he sold his expertise in crime, and sold it well, and behaved in real war chief. To where in the daytime when things turned to carnage and they killed a dozen police officers who held a dam to control the vehicles passing the border between Bolivia and Colombia. These "idiots" had threatened to seize their goods. " But who do they think they are?," he had told his men before asking them to leave their weapons and take care of these louts.

Once again, his excessive zeal displeased his employers. But these, knowing that it would be foolish to dispense with this crazy determination, this taste for the murder, decided to keep him away. I was lucky because in Miami, Griselda Blanco was facing increasingly exacerbated competition on the part of the Cuban gang who had formed and she asked for help to confront these Chicanos who were the violent type. Pablo Escobar Gaviria, who seemed to have taken the upper hand over their other associates, so sent him this crime expert.

When he entered her, Griselda noticed the look cold and determined the man. She explained her worries, pointed the guilty, and asked him to act with energy.

«Don't worry not, Ms. Blanco...

-Call me Griselda, she interrupts him.

- And you can call me Riverito, said in his turn.

- And in our group, everyone is familiar.

-You are looking, he continues with difficulty because, as a former military, he didn't used to name his superiors, someone who is not afraid to face determined opponents. And I can tell you that when you're dealing with guerrillas in a hostile jungle, you better you struggle without waiting for God's help.

-How many men will take you? She asked just in case.

-For the moment any, Griselda. I just arrived and the time that I'm familiarizing myself with the places, I prefer to act alone. The needs I have at the moment

114

is to have the weapons and the ammunition to make the job.

"- Request and you'll have everything you need."

Jorge Ayala gave her a list of weapons which she knew names after hearing them in the movies which she liked. Griselda knew then that her friends not laughed of her.

The next day, Jorge Riverito Ayala began support to accomplish the mission for which we had come to Miami. As her boss told him he touch a bonus to each corpse and that, according to the importance of the Maccabees, it would be more or less important. To support an already exaggerated zeal.

The first to die were those called the "Marielitos". These men were originating from the city of Mariel in Cuba and which were made to a place in the "Little Havana" neighborhood, on the back of their rivals by sending them all "ad patres". Moreover, these rogue junk, as Ayala had dubbed them, were easy to recognize because they were made to be tattooed a tear at the corner of the right eye. Thus, it was enough to cross them in the street to recognize them. He thus slew those who sold drugs on the sidewalks before tackling those who had settled in bars. After a week, the toll was heavy: he had killed eleven of these Cubans. The two brothers who were board of leaders, then decided to enter the dance.

They led investigation and were told who had killed all their men acted alone. An informant told them even the place where the man lived, a motel in the Westchester neighborhood, in west of the city. A reprisal expedition was immediately organized. A convoy of four cars, with five men on aboard each of her, joined towards the destination. Upon arrival in the parking lot of the motel, men went down and surrendered in the room that had given them the owner of the motel under the threat of their weapons. Ten killers burst into the room occupied by Jorge Ayala, paving the way for their two leaders who wanted to take care personally of this jerk. But thirty seconds after entering, an explosion occurred and killed all the Cubans present in the apartment. As more than the boss of the motel had warned police that landed and took care of those who stayed and who did not hesitate to shoot against police cars. The toll was heavy: Twelve men killed by the explosion and seven others killed by police. The gang of the "Marielitos" not recovered.

When he came to his report to Griselda, Jorge Riverito Ayala returned with a wad of forty-one thousand dollars. Thousand dollars per man and ten thousand for each of the both leaders. The killer is not returned. He had never been rewarded in this way. His zeal became even more exacerbated. So much so that to fulfill his mission, or rather his missions because rival gangs were not lacking, he asked permission, which could not that be granted to build a team of sicarios. He brought one of the men with whom he had shared stocks commandos in the Colombian jungle. The man's name was Miguel Perez. Upon his arrival, the right-hand man of Jorge Riverito Ayala formed, he too, his group of killers who did not hesitate to act considering, in one thousand dollars the murder, that the work was very well paid.

Therefore, the corpses mounted. To the point that the morgues and funeral services of the police came running out of room to store the bodies of men found on part of the city. A death in four had fallen under the bullets. The police chief then decided to rent refrigerated trucks that the Burger King Company used to transport goods between its burgers manufacturing plant and its many fast foods.

The gunshot homicide rate tripled in less than two years. Before the proliferation of these murders, the press began to compare the Miami of the 1980s at the Chicago of the 1920s s. These killers were nicknamed by the press: "Cocaine Cowboys." General insecurity became problematic, and the authorities were bound to act. Because the murders were taking place everywhere and there is not a mall where rival gangs did not hesitate to confront, even in daylight, the light and full. The climate of impunity was such that one day, Miguel Perez, in person, murdered a gang leader in the Miami airport before a crowd of witnesses, stabbing him with a bayonet. This could not continue. It was time for this to stop.

FIRST FLAWS

It took her three years to achieve, but Griselda had cleaned up around her. From his penthouse in Miami, she organized the elimination of all rivals. Now, no one dared to step on her toes, knowing assent. She could now thrive in peace. The million mounted and, according to some, his fortune now exceeded $ 1 billion. What let her free from the need for several generations.

But this success was to change his way of life. She had been high bottle that her mother sometimes filled with brandy on the pretext that it was healthier to put polluted water bringing diseases, began to taste this white powder that Americans were in the nostrils. And like them, she discovered the benefits of this virtuous plant that was the coke. Because she took taste.

Because business is good and her team, led by Jorge Riverito Ayala, kept a close watch, she could finally rest and have a good time. She was a Cuban masseur, handsome, muscular and tanned, which made her massage sessions who became special. This Hidalgo afforded her such a pleasure that he became her official lover. But as Cuban, he couldn't settle for being the lover of this chunky woman of a fifty meter two. And although the sexual appetite of this woman of forty years ago was insatiable, he convinced her to organize parties for her friends and to bring strippers and gogo-dancers to set the mood and heat the spirits. And for those who were not satisfied with their presence where they showed themselves in the air swayed disco music, they put them at disposal of the white powder filled bowls where straws

were willing to allow them to sniff all the cocaine they wanted.

The parties multiplied and Griselda, who became increasingly paranoid by the dint of cocaine, fell into this lethargy leading criminals to disengage from their business. Which was what they called the beginning of the end for people that only crime motivated. Not to be outdone, and that her associates worried, she gave more responsibility to Jorge Riverito Ayala. She commissioned him to do the dirty work and to motivate him, increased its dividends. Now, she considered him a partner, provided who he ensures that Miami dealers who worked for them do their share of work. Because it was not enough to provide of cocaine; He also had to sell it. It was also reported that the most. Then misfortune to those who did not make enough figure and did not fill by their working part. From what was said, the network of Griselda Blanco had a thousand of small dealers. And she fed them with her friends of Medellin who weren't idle to provide the growing demand.

But American authorities had decided to act and had put pressure on the heads of law enforcement to fight drug trafficking. The DEA flow a special agent to identify and bring down the most important network of cocaine. The man's name was Robert Palombo. He was not a novice on the subject and was fighting against the traffic of cocaine for years. It was he who had led the operation in New York on the Hudson River in 1976 against the network of Griselda, called the Bravo network, and had failed to arrest her former husband, Alberto, after having had information by a man of the Miami's Godfather, Santo Traficcante

Junior, he was arrested in Florida. Vindictive, the man threw himself headlong into this investigation and accumulated information.

Meanwhile, Griselda, who had settled the account of his Cuban masseur after seeing him flirt with a stripper, was the meeting of a new Hidalgo that she fell in love, Dario Sepulveda. The man was a Colombian trafficker who operated in United States and who had come to meet her, at the request of her associates of Medellin, to learn from the experience of this that was beginning to nickname it "the Queen of cocaine." But their meeting took a different turn. Love at first sight between them was mutual. They liked each other immediately and soon became lovers. Dario Sepulveda cradled her then love and made her forget her taste for partying, but especially for cocaine.

He settled in her penthouse and gave her all the pleasure that she asked him. So much so that she got pregnant again. Of her fourth child. She had not forgotten three others who worked for her friends in Medellin. But this one, it'd be something else. She felt like that. Especially since Dario and she had wed in a marriage. When she gave birth, she called her son Michael Corleone. Because she had become a huge fan of the Francis Ford Coppola film, "The godfather". His son so wearing that name that was, for her, a sense that she was the only one to understand. The days continued in found happiness. But it was always an end.

Griselda and Dario were happy. They were both crazy in love, but there's that Dario was homesick for the country. He did not of this life, that he knew and more risky, and proposed to his wife to return to live in Colombia in a

nice area of Bogota where he found that the air was healthier and the climate was better. Not to mention that to convince her, he said that their situation was special and he was afraid that one day or another, the police don't come in their apartment and put an end to this fantastic life. Griselda tried to reason with him by explaining that their situation was fabulous and that never, where anything, they would have a better life. Their different point of life ushered in a disagreement that worsened over time.

No way for her to leave her penthouse and this gigantic terrace that overlooked the sea and where she could see the sunrise and the sunset. She knew, she, how it had been a long road and how life had been hard until she could enjoy such an existence. She knew the misfortunes she had known and what she had to make to overcome the difficulties of life. Now that happiness was there, she would never resolve to give it up. And certainly not to return to Colombia, the country where she had experienced so much misery.

But as the days went by and more their different is accentuated. Their intimate relationship deteriorated to the point that they did not make practically anymore love. They had to go to the obvious: they loved more and had to decide to put an end to their relationship. A divorce seemed inevitable. But she would agree to a divorce only on one condition. Then before that Dario leaves the marital home, she warned.

"If you walk out of my life, you better move away from me because I can't bear to see making out you with another woman."

But there was more to have Dario Sepulveda fear. His wife might be the Queen of cocaine, he needed him

121

more to tremble. In fact, he was Colombian and had also made a career in drug trafficking. So it wasn't this woman in a little more than a fifty meter that would intimidate him. He decided to return to Colombia, but he refused to leave empty-handed. So he decided to act.

The day came, he pretended to take his son to a mall for him a gift. Griselda was wary and warned him.

"If you're not back in two hours, I send my dogs after asking them to rip your balls off!"

Dario Sepulveda was not scared. He had planned the suite and made sure that everything happens as he had organized it. As soon as he left the building, he took over direction of the airport where he took a direct flight to Bogota.

Two hours later, her husband and her son had still not returned. Griselda was irritated. She called Jorge Riverito Ayala and asked him to begin the search. The evening, still no news. She went into a mad rage and began to break everything in his apartment that belonged to Dario. It was not until she had destroyed everything, she calmed. She had to go to the evidence. Dario's never coming back. Didn't matter it, in fact, let it go. But what she doesn't bore, is let to ridicule her in this way. Not only to have been having as a debutante, but mostly because her future ex-husband had taken her son unless she has doubts about whether. She wanted to punish him. Not only that he died. She wanted that he suffers and he asks forgiveness.

A few days later, Griselda learned that Dario and his son, Michael Corleone, was spotted in the airport. They were gone in a plane of the company Avianca for Bogota.

This seemed logical because it was there that he wanted to return to live. She now knew where to look. So she called her friends, and God knows they were many in Colombia, and asked them to find him. But she demanded that he be taken alive and let it be done to him suffer the worst punishment.

A week just so that those who were looking for find him. He lived in a luxury apartment in downtown where security guards provided surveillance. So, no way to capture him. A mill was set up and a few days later, Dario Sepulveda was killed while he was at the wheel of his car by the fake policemen in a barrage of identity check who wanted to force him to shut down the engine. They had no choice, because by knowing that it was fake policemen, he had used his weapon to force the dam. Fortunately, these men had made attention so it is does no harm to the child who was sitting at his side. Michael Corleone was recovered and put on a plane to be returned to his mother, Griselda, who found her son a few days later. And she also found a smile. She had suffered had to be separated from her three sons when Carlos Trujillo put her out. Michael Corleone, his youngest, will never be removed him. She vowed that taking him in his arms and stroking her hair.

Griselda went back to life, under the gaze of his son, who did not dare to ask about his father. She had stopped partying, even if it wasn't envy that she lacked. But she didn't want her son to be the witness of too much debauchery, as she had been seeing his mother bring men home to copulate.

In Miami, the business continued. And his henchmen continued to kill men who disputed their authority. For their part, American authorities were on the teeth. French Connection no longer existed and the sharp decline in the use of heroin in United States, replaced by this other white powder was cocaine, caused a redistribution of the cards. The fight against cocaine trafficking became the priority of all DEA agents. DEA made his priority. As in Miami, the corpses did not cease to pile up in morgues.

Ordered by the Government which had declared the war against drug trafficking, DEA decided to put all means. She took advantage of a tension between the two most important Boss of Cosa Nostra, Santo Traficcante Junior and John Gotti, to increase pressure on this latter representing the four great New York families. The witness protection program was largest funding in place to ensure that languages are loosened. Thus, those who wanted to take me out of the crime began to speak. This became a complex because everyone criticized everyone in exchange for a safe bet.

Robert Palombo, always based in Miami and working hard on the Blanco case, multiplied investigations and accumulated charges against this powerful network, not to say the most powerful networks. But his research proved to be sterile because whenever he neared the goal, those that he was about to stop were eliminated. So much so that he began to wonder if it was a mole in his service. It was true that the Queen of cocaine had a lot of money and she knew to use them wisely. So he sought on the side of tax authorities by saying he could possibly set her up, as Eliot Ness had managed to make with Al Capone. After all, journalists cease to say that Miami looked like in Chicago of the prohibition. But he would get, on that side too, he found nothing that allows him to charge Griselda Blanco.

In fact, she behaved even as a benefactor and showed great generosity to the orphans of Miami. Even if some of them were orphans because of the actions of his assassins. Griselda, who had not forgotten the misery of his childhood, financed orphanages in Miami to Cuban and Puerto Rican youth. Just as her associates of Medellin did for Colombian children of the streets. She did it by empathy, in contrast to her friends who were doing that with an ulterior motive by saying that once adolescents or adults, they dedicated men, body and soul, to put themselves at the service of their benefactors. The idea was not new. She had always been used by those who knew that the best of the recognitions was on a full stomach.

Griselda continued her quiet life far day where she made the acquaintance of a Cuban whose she not resisted the charm. She was approaching midlife, she was always a woman needs to satisfy. And even if she was bought a moral for not that her son suffers, she decided to make her lover. Even if their first meetings were made outside her apartment. After all, it wasn't luxury hotels lacking in Miami.

But what she didn't know, was this Hidalgo was, in fact, a narcotics agent who had received for mission to infiltrate her network. And how is he, amazed his superiors. What better way to set up a member of the underworld to sneak into his bed.

Before deciding to infiltrate an agent who would take such risks, Robert Palombo sought all means to bring down that which, for him, represented what he hated most. At the same time a drug dealer who is enriched by taking advantage of human misery, but also a person who used these fortune to commit crimes in braving the justice. He had so that found a way to make her fall: the flagrante delicto. But as it was not she who was directly engaged in traffic, there is no way to make this. He therefore decided to take the risk to infiltrate an agent, with what it was. And that's his agent came to seduce that he wanted to throw it down at all costs. Since the worm was in the fruit, the trap could close.

The Cuban lover of Griselda began to sniff cocaine, as did his mistress. Except that he did not have. He will then offer the bags of cocaine by pleading a need for his personal consumption. And this gift made under the eye of a camera that filmed the entire scene. The trap was closed.

One morning, as she did regularly, both conscious of being safe and oblivious to the threat that hung over it, sure that no one would go for it, but ignorant of the number of enemies who would like to shot her, she left to make her shopping spree in the Dadeland Mall where she made herself drop by her driver. She ran through the aisles, stopped in many shops and bought everything that tried it, clothing and accessories brand, which she had no need but because she loved to pretend all these stuck-up who spent just to show their bags, signs of wealth. If only they knew these floozies that Griselda had much more money that a life could be enough to spend.

Unfortunately for her, more busy staring at these women much more attractive than her, she didn't notice the pairs of eyes on her and who did not leave her a second. As she got out of the Gallery to access another, Jaime Bravo, one of the many nephews of her ex-husband Alberto, who had escaped the vendetta against his family putting himself at the service of the Ochoa family, and a handful of accomplices came out of a van, weapons in hand, to liquidate when the Ochoa family members its former partners, wanted to make the skin. They made this decision because, although doing business together, she had killed one of their nieces who owed her five hundred thousand dollars, a small fee for them who were part of the Medellin cartel and who were rich in millions, not to tell in billions. And more as partners, she should never have to make that.

Fortunately for her, Robert Palombo was, too, on the scene to arrest her. When one of his officers rang the alarm when approaching the Group of killers, he gave his men the order to intervene. The minutes which followed saw unfold an irrational scene. Men armed with automatic weapons found themselves face to face and set plays, each threatening the others. The tension came to a head and it took few things for guns spit their murderous fire and causes a real carnage. This funny scene happened under the eyes of Griselda who understood that something unusual was happening. Without asking her rest, she took advantage that the killers and the police were always together not eyes to slip away.

Griselda came to understand two things: first, that she was under surveillance by the police and secondly, that of the killers followed her but them, for settle her account. She quickly returned to her penthouse, filed in her room, opened the safe that was there and took the bundles of notes that she had stored there. She had no choice. As it happened there was a dozen years, she had to flee, urgently, before the police raided her home. Most importantly, since the police were on his trail, she had to hide in a place where they would not find. And this place, she was the only one to know.

At least, she thought.

NEW LIFE

Before leaving this apartment where she had spent good moments, Griselda spent a last phone call. She called the one which was the only one she trusted again, Jorge Riverito Ayala. She explained to him what had happened and ended with these words:

"Now, you're the boss of the network but I ask to you to pay me 10% of what you earn. Another thing, beware because the cops are on our tracks. So to you to arrange to not make you take. And finally, I ask you to take care of my son and take him to a place where he will not be threatened. Because I'm sure that those who wanted to kill me, going to come at him to force me out of my hole. I shall contact you when I shall be under cover. I'll tell you where to send my son and give him for travel bag, money that comes back to me. "Vaya Con Dios".

Which meant: Godspeed, in Spanish.

She then went directly to the central station and took a train to Tampa, a travel bag for only piece of luggage. But inside, she's had piled up $ 2 million. What bounce. Once in this city, she took a bus, a long time that she not had, up to New Orleans. Once in the capital of Louisiana, she went to Houston, in Texas and, this time, she decided to take air plane. That's two days that she was traveling without sleep lest we stole her bag, only fortune and only trace of his omnipotence that remained.

She arrived in the airport of Los Angeles, in California, where her mother, Anna Lucia, lived. She got in a taxi and took place in the latino neighborhood where she lived in a modest bungalow. Despite the fortune of her daughter, she would never take advantage of the financial windfall of her criminal activities when she left Colombia to remake her life in a country where a woman was not forced to prostitute to earn money to eat. But she was also gone when she had known what activities indulged her daughter. Shame that resulted was far too important to accept it. Then one day, advised by the mother superior of the religious institution where she had stayed after getting there clean, she was gone to the city with this sweet name 'Nuestra Señora de Los Angeles', our Lady of angels. That's a nice name where she could rebuild her life and draw a line under his past.

But what Ana Lucia didn't know was that it was her daughter who had everything arranged to allow her to rebuild a future. It was she who had given money to the religious institution so that she keeps her during these years, she who had given money to the mother superior that she convinces her to leave Colombia and go to another country where she knew people who could take care of her, she who had obtained her the visa of emigration, she who had paid bribes to get the famous Green Card , the green card which allowed to work in United States, who had financed the American institution for support and find her a home and a job in a safe area but where people spoke Spanish. This district was Irvine, a suburb in south of Los Angeles where lived a strong Hispanic community.

When Griselda stood in her doorway, she refused to open her. But she insisted, and found the words to make her understand what had happened to her since her departure of Medellin, she owed it to her. And to convince her, she quoted her the names of all the people who are were occupied with her since the day where she took her in this religious institution.

"We know, you and me, how it is hard for a woman in Colombia to know happiness. I've watched over you, mother, as I have watched over my three boys that I was forbidden to see. I made sure they never experience hunger and I think I managed. Since the day when my first husband threw me out, I swore that never, never again, I won't let a man manage my life. Then you might have heard some abominations on me, but I didn't make me respect by these men who did not see in me that a piece of bacon to one meter fifty all just good to be stuffed! "

After thirty minutes to listen her daughter, Ana Lucia consented to open the door. But when she spoke to her daughter, it was to ask her conditions. She led a quiet life and would tolerate no misconduct. Griselda's answer was to take her mother in arms and to tell her some words the ear.

"Never, mother, never I don't will any harm, any hurt. You too suffered in your life so that I add to the misfortune. "

Griselda moved so in the small room that her mother used to store things that she had no usefulness but that could, one day, maybe. The first days, she merely watching television and track information. They still spoke numerous settlings of scores which took place in Miami. Few imported for her, it did not concern her any more. On the other hand, she followed with interest series of events that were happening in Florida. The series was called "Miami Vice".

After a month in hiding and to make sure nobody had followed her, Griselda decided to call Jorge Riverito Ayala. She told him the place where he had to bring his son and where she would send someone to get him back. She was afraid that the killers who had wanted to liquidate her do not follow her and succeed in finding her track. Thus she would go get him in San Francisco. There, she would take a train to Las Vegas where she would take him to sow any pursuers before renting a taxi to return to Los Angeles. When mother and son arrived in the bungalow, Ana Lucia could not only be submerged by discovering his last grandson that she did not know. The family was finally reunited. Even if it missed the others three boys. But they lived in Colombia and were installed in Medellin. When we knew what was happening, as much as they are, said Anna Lucia to Griselda.

The days passed quietly. Griselda wanted her mother stop to work. She had come with two million dollars, a sum he would need ten lives to win. Not to mention what Michael Corleone brought in his small suitcase with wheels. Jorge Riverito Ayala had kept his word and gave $ 10 million to her son. "This is what buy you another penthouse at the edge of the Pacific ocean", he had marked on a small paper. No, she wouldn't do the same mistake by being exposed. She preferred to remain in this bungalow where there were hot but who at least had the merit of protect them from those who were looking for. The mother and the son remained there, expect that things settle down enjoying the good food that Grandma used to make them and who smelled Colombia.

The days passed and the three members of the Blanco family celebrated the new year. We were in 1985. Things seemed to be packed. Griselda and Michael Corleone took advantage of their new life and took good time thanks to the money she had side. But Robert Palombo returned in the part. Those who seek to bring down the Queen of cocaine for ten years, had never let go. Griselda Blanco was his main goal and he would never stop until he would not arrested her and wouldn't rest until he would have put her under lock and key.

By means of doggedness, his investigations eventually yield results. After months of surveillance, stakeouts and wiretaps, he manages to follow the trail up to her back. Thanks Jaime Bravo, who knew that the Medellin cartel, who had already left him once life save wouldn't give a second chance. His only way to stay alive was to collaborate with the police to take advantage of the Act on the Protection of Witnesses. He began to speak, and taught him that Griselda had a mother who lived in California. On the other hand, he did not know where. But what better place to hide than the city that mattered more than latinos: Los Angeles.

The time that the operation is put in place, there was no urgency because target flowed quiet days, DEA and FBI agents arrived near the bungalow in the middle of the night of February 20 and took positions all around to be sure, this time, she does not escape. Robert Palombo couldn't take it. So that as soon as everyone was in place, he gave the order to launch the assault. The agents did not lace. Using their ram, they cut doors and windows, and officers rushed inside through what the bungalow was like opening. Griselda was quietly sleeping in her bed, lying near her son. She let herself understand without resisting for fear that her son Michael, who had seen his father die before his eyes, is once more traumatized. After all, even getting caught, might as well be by the police rather than by the killers who would not hesitate to killer her mother and her son. She reassured her son and her mother and told them that everything would be alright while they passed her handcuffs and told her his rights.

But there was more to impress her. As soon as she was outside, away from the gaze of hers, she spoke to an agent and asked:

"Who is your chief?

- It's me! Threw Robert Palombo in eying her gaze. It's been a while that I'm on your tracks, you know? I almost have you in New York ten years ago. But I had to wait. Today, it's me you're lucky. "

Griselda barely listened, approached him unless he backs up, and kissed him on the mouth before there was time to sketch the slightest gesture. Two inspectors held her yet. But they had not seen it coming, certainly not expecting this.

"After having managed to escape in New York, I swore to my ex-husband to kiss on the mouth this would happen to handcuff me. It's done. I kept the promise I made him! "

The police could not help to hold back a laugh. Not only because they thought it was cheeky, but also because the Chief came to be embraced by a woman of one meter fifty two and sixty-eight pounds. Not really a mannequin. It was true that Griselda had spent all those months watching TV to snack on sweet things and eat ice cream to the soup spoon.

Meanwhile, the police took her under heavy guard on the premises of the Los Angeles police. She was interrogated and denied altogether what was alleged against her. Bundles of bank notes that they had found in the bungalow: "The savings of a lifetime of work to my mother and me", dared to say. The money was seized the time that the investigation continues. Fortunately she had placed a large part in the trunk of a bank before her mother and her son are free from want.

As she was threatened, Robert Palombo decided to put her in a secret place hoping that she speaks. So much for her civil rights. Later, she would speak to a lawyer.

But Griselda could not be put to the secret too long. Robert Palombo was a head of DEA, he had to respect the law. So that after ninety-six hours in custody, he locked her up in a special cell in a high security zone. He knew that, at least, she was safe. But the information eventually leaked. And as soon as she reached the ears of journalists, media, making fat cabbages with the waves of crimes of Miami, seized of this case that would let them sell, again, a lot of paper. Therefore, the editions of newspapers increased and passed the new loop on the radio and TV stations: 'the woman so-called 'Cocaïne Queen' had been arrested in Los Angeles. '

Those who hated her could not but rejoice, even if some would prefer to see her dead. American authorities congratulated the police action. But as was always the case for those who had, one day, the headlines, that admirers became known and incensed this woman who was only a fifty meter and who, nevertheless, was imposed in this environment where many criminals had left life. This woman was, for those who had nothing and who would like to have his fortune, a real Idol. Because it was not possible that this little woman could make this type of business without the benefit of a gift of nature and intellectual faculties that were an exceptional being.

The reporters saw a way to make headlines. They had a vested interest to maintain the legend to continue to sell paper and spots of advertising. That is that one of the journalists, the competition raged. So much so that some of them wondered if this woman was not good sense out of the ordinary to turn the spirits. Those who benefited from contacts within the FBI or DEA sought to glean information. You then spoke to them of this woman who would have sold hundreds of kilos of cocaine while leading a life of quiet mother in a miserable bungalow.

THE AFTER LIFE

But among those who cared about the "Cocaine Queen", only those who lived on drug trafficking incensed her while others hated her basis as the revelations were made. Among those who admired her, there was a certain Charles Cosby. A boy of eighteen who lived in a poor suburb of the East of Oakland and who made himself its crystals of crack in his home to sell them. He might be a neighborhood dealer, he had a shabby, all existence by selling his ten stones a week.

For him, this woman was a real Queen. Besides, it wasn't for nothing that was nicknamed "Cocaïne Queen". As thousands of people and hundreds of dealers, he was interested in the subject that he came to take of admiration for this woman that journalists were as a strange and surprising phenomenon. Captivating and intriguing. The qualifiers were not lacking to journalists to describe her. And as the information was distilled, because he didn't tell everything too fast and she was surprised more those who followed what they told her.

If Charles made his main topic of discussion, his friends refused to believe what they called a legend made by journalists just to sell paper.

"How could a woman be at the head of the largest network of import and sale of cocaine. They denounced.

-Why not! " Insisted Charles who wanted to believe what his friends said.

Fascinated by the subject, Charles began to buy all newspapers which spoke of Griselda Blanco. And as it satisfied not to quench his thirst, he devoted time, plenty of time to watch TV to see, and even review, newspapers which spoke of Griselda. And here's the ABC television channel revealed that his fortune was estimated at two billion dollars by some experts. What good fan of lusts. Charles is more impassioned for the 'Cocaine Queen' and spent day and night thinking about this fabulous treasure. To such a point that a morning, an idea crossed her mind: and if he was going to meet her in prison. He ruminated this crazy idea that began to obsess him and virtually never got out of his memory. Until the day or, a morning, he decided: "I want to see her." He washed his as he had not done it for a long time, put on his clothes more fashionable, and took a bus to downtown Dublin. It was there that was the prison.

The prison for women in Dublin was thirty-five kilometers from Oakland. Griselda had been incarcerated because the judge had refused the release bail requested by his lawyers. They had however proposed to the Attorney general to pay a huge deposit to support the decision, but this was unsuccessful. As far as she had left the country ten years ago to escape an arrest and a possible indictment, the judge had preferred to lock her up to be sure that, this time, she cannot escape. The release bail was refused her so.

Charles Crosby, him, went to prison and presented himself at the reception where he asked to meet with Griselda Blanco. It fulfills the prescribed form but, after a wait of an hour in a room where the Director of the prison and his assistants watched him to room height, they notified him a refusal to visit. The warden explained while only members of family of the prisoners were allowed to meet them.

He was disappointed and then returned home, invaded by a form of anxiety that ended his dream. Once home, he threw himself on his bed without even bothering to remove his clothes strung with care. He remained a part of the evening, eyes lost in the scope of his ceiling. He thought about a way to meet what he considered a real Idol. He hoped so this meeting, and said that with his experience, she could benefit from his knowledge, provide his expertise so that he becomes, like her, a cocaine Lord, a true champion of the dope. He says so he took at his own game and began to create contacts with the "Cocaine Queen". And he told everyone to believe, in him to others, he was one of his relationships.

And that is that one day, a woman who had worked for several years for Griselda, came into contact with him.

"It appears you've got contacts with Griselda Blanco?" She asked him.

Charles Cosby tried to tell him so gross nonsense that he came to get lost in his explanations.

"Listen boy, cut her annoyed by his hazy explanations that only a deaf person would believe. I don't know what you're trying to tell me, but I think tell me stories. So stop telling me Bull! "

Charles understood that he wouldn't have to convince this woman. Then as he no longer knew what to say and was even out of pitch, a last straw for him was not his tongue in his pocket and who had fooled more than one, he made her his secret.

"The truth is I admire this woman! He said. I don't know... but I admire her! When I see all that she has done for years without the cops her stuck...

- So, you know or you don't know?

- No, unfortunately, I don't know, he confessed. But I have so much admiration for her... This woman is a true Queen, although she is only a Queen of cocaine. One day, I even took the bus to her prison to meet her. But they wouldn't let me do. But one day, I will return. And if we still refuse me, I will return again. Until they let me see her!

- You know that there is a whole bunch of people who want to shut her down?

- No... But it's not what I want to make. What I want, me, is to meet her. I want she teach me everything she knows of this profession. That's what I want!

- In any case, if you don't know, me, I know! She threw him to know his reaction

- You know you?

- Yes boy, I know her!

- You know where?

- I've worked long for her.

- Oh yes, and what did you make to her?

- I worked for years for her.

- By doing what? Business or household?

- You are Moron! It's because I'm a woman you say that?

- Sorry, that's not what I meant! he resumed, seeing that the girl was beginning to get excited.

- I've been called a mule!

- You were thought of some the drug for her?

- Yes, boy! And for years. And not the small bags as you're selling! Me, I spent three pounds a week. A kilo two pounds on belly and breasts!

- I can't believe you? You want to explain? "

The woman called Marta. She did the mule for Griselda Blanco for years. Every Monday, she was leaving by plane from Bogota to land in New York. She spent a kilo of cocaine divided in pockets sewn into her bra, and two other kilos in a sheath she wore to the belt. She then took a taxi to the latino neighborhood and deposited her goods in a hotel room where she was spending the night, all expenses paid. The next day, she took a flight to Miami, where she found a contact who gave her a sum of money that she brought back by plane to her Boss of Bogota. She did the same thing each week using a passport with a different identity.

Their discussion continued for many minutes and exchanges of experience were not missing. To the extent that they met several times until their meetings take a sexual connotation. After several days of meetings of legs in the air, Marta decided to please her young stud. She promised to talk about him to Griselda who she took money in jail to allow her to pay for what improve her comfort and especially enough to ensure her safety.

During one of her visits, Marta told her about this young man who admired her and considered her as a real

Idol. Griselda was first surprised, then was wary, before convincing someone can be considered as a Queen. Who could be that young man scraping dealer rocks of crack in his neighborhood in San Francisco? But the way Marta talked about him, she realized they were lovers. Maybe he was a good shot? She wondered. Then she tells her to thank them for this appreciation and convey her sympathy.

Then over the weeks, an idea came to her in mind. So that during the next visit of Marta, she gave her the phone number of the visiting room of the prison in Dublin.

"I'll tell you a mission, she said. You're going to memorize this number and tell this boy call me at ten o'clock. But above all, what he always calls from a phone box. Don't call me ever from home! Tell him that regardless of the day, I'll be by the phone," explained to Marta hoping she would not yield to jealousy.

You never knew with this kind of women. But Marta, who knew what was able Griselda Blanco, fulfills its mission and gave the phone number to Charles in explaining him the recommendations she had given her.

Charles Cosby came not back when Marta gave him the phone number. He scored it on a piece of paper and note also the instructions of Griselda. Finally, he was able to speak with her. It was as if he was in communication with a person of the afterlife. Immediately, the next day, Charles went at 9:30 to the nearest payphone from where he lived. He stood next to the cabin and made the crane foot. At ten o'clock on the dot, he called her.

"Hello, I would like to talk to Griselda Blanco", he mumbles, after having struggled to find his words.

He waited a few seconds and then heard in the telephone handset, a voice that seemed to come from far, not to say of the afterlife:

"Griselda Blanco to the phone. Who can wonder? "

Overcome with emotion, he was seized with a feeling of happiness. Finally, he spoke with his idol. Their conversation lasted a few minutes. But the happiness that drew out Charles Cosby was so strong that he had as a pleasurable impression. As if he had made love. He had to make a superhuman effort to agree to hang up the telephone handset. Still spur of the moment, he stood there for long seconds, looking at the phone, and wondering if he had not dreamed. He remembered what was said during their exchange and resumed his spirits to be recalled what she had told him. He then returned home, dragging his feet because constantly prey to the disorder. Once in his room, he took a sheet of paper and wrote what she had told him. First to do not forget the advice, but also for power reread what he regarded as divine words. Finally, what were the words spoken by the Queen of cocaine.

He took a second sheet and added some things he wanted to talk to her the next day. He knew that the phone might be tapped, then he would have to find images, parables as saying specialists, to grill.

But when it came the next day, he had no time to place in it one because Griselda, who talked nonstop, did not leave the time. She knew that the police were listening to his conversation. Then she spoke words hidden and told Charles to things that he had trouble understanding. It was only when he wrote what she had told him on sheets of paper that he knew then that they were coded messages. The next day, he called her again and came to drag her to write her to express admiration that he bore her. She paused to think about it and told him it was a great idea. But beware, should not forget that the mail was opened.

It was as well as their correspondence began. First a few leaves and then, after a few weeks, they were genuine declaration of love she received. Her femininity, in lack of love, could no longer. It has been months that she had had no orgasm. That had left so life if, deprived of liberty, she couldn't even more send in the air and take her foot. So to maintain her desires and be satisfied alone, she asked him to send her pictures of him. Griselda was seduced by his unknown. Not by this kid who idolized her but because in his letters were genuine declarations of love that Charles sent her. She, started moping and indulge in melancholy. She wrote to him that his days were also sad that depressing and as long as boring. To restore morale, Charles replied that he had taken of passion for her, he would never cease to write her.

Griselda could not it any more. She who was in need of love and who had not received a mark of affection for a long time, asked him to come and see. She told him she would arrange for that, this time, access is not denied. Charles was overjoyed. Happiness, as he never had, presented to him. And, soon to celebrate his twenty years. What more beautiful birthday gift could hope?

But Dublin prison was under strong surveillance as authorities expect everything from the men of the "Cocaine Queen". When we knew what they were capable, the prison management was expecting what they attempt the impossible to make escape and avoid years in prison waiting for her. As Robert Palombo had not finished with her. As long as she had not been sentenced by justice, he continued his investigations before she takes the heaviest sentences.

Besides, although the Queen of cocaine is in jail, the network was still active under the cup of Jorge Riverito Ayala, who continued the business and caused millions of dollars of recipe. And even if the Medellin cartel had decided to no longer work with her when she did murder a niece of the Ochoa family, at the instigation of Griselda, he had established contacts with a small cartel who was waiting to grow, the Cali cartel. So while traffic continued and the imaginary family members visited her, ready to all risks to send her money in jail.

She did well as Medellin, things had become terrible for leaders who made up the cartel. These men who were out of the poor suburbs had become rich businessmen to millions, not to say billion thanks to an uncommon intelligence. Their fortune had trained them in a kind of megalomania which did not accept that it opposes them. They were allies, consciously or not, to criminals, the M19 guerrillas, then to right-wing militias. To continue their traffic, they had collaborated with the Cuban authorities, in lack of currency from the greed of the new Soviet leader Michael Gorbachev. Their ships would stop in the island of Cuba, which served as relay, before resuming the navigation up to the southern tip of Florida. They had also negotiated with the revolutionaries of the Nicaragua and the dictator of the Panama whence their planes could take off to ensure the Drop, the deliveries of cocaine, to Florida via Cuba or the Andros Island in Bahamas.

After having infiltrated all Colombian institutions through corruption allowed by their "Pedrodollars", the leaders of the Medellin cartel had reached a power without limit. But now that the new Colombian authorities disputed their power. They had then decided to respond with violence, imposing terror on the country sinking into a form of paranoia murdered. Death by murder became the leading cause of death, far superior to the disease and traffic accidents together.

Griselda who knew he was threatened, was made to ensure her security. In prison, she paid a rent of two thousand dollars per month in order to occupy a cell alone. And she was paying up to $ 10,000 so that women, who had been incarcerated near her cell, watch over her. And they were not contenders that were missing.

A NEW LOVE

The day where Charles Cosby would be able to meet his idol had come. For the occasion, he was adorned with his best stuff. Not those that he was wearing when she first came because he couldn't find enough beautiful. Then, he had spent his remaining money to buy a suit, used of course, but a suit anyway. When he entered prison, he again fills the form but, this time, they did not wait. As soon as the procedure applied, he was introduced in a visiting room. As if by magic, they were alone in the visiting room, which is usually crowded with people. It was true that Griselda, who wanted to meet alone with the one who was going to give her a pleasure as she had not had for a long time, had distributed $100 bills so that no prisoner makes her family come this day there.

Charles entered the room and forward, trembling legs, up to a table where Griselda was installed. As soon as he was within her reach, she rose, approached him and kissed him on the mouth as if it was his first kiss. There was a long time that Charles was not entitled to a kiss as passionate and languorous. And the kiss lasted for a time that never ends. It was only when the air came to miss her, Griselda gave him back his mouth.

"It's been so long that I didn't kiss a man! Threw to be sitting down again, a smile ecstatic to the lips.

- And me, it's been a long time that a woman has not kissed me this way, he muttered, not knowing what to say.

- So, how do look me? Am I the image you were me? She asked.

- You're good to the image I had of you!

- It's a shame that we are not alone! She said letting go in love with smile.

- The opportunity arises, he said, blushing.

- You're right, we will have other opportunities. And I will undertake to ensure that this happens as best as possible. So tell me, told me you wanted me to teach you some things?

- You're the Queen of cocaine. The one who knows all the tricks. So, I want to learn all of this business. The craft, matter, and what you should know.

- Before I tell you what anyone, tell me about yourself. "

Charles Cosby explained to her his life. He told how he bought big rocks of Crack that he cut to sell them in his neighborhood.

"And how much get you out of your business? She asked him.

- To live without starving. Of course I can win more, but I guess out of the area and take more risk.

- The Crack is not what pays the most. How would take for you to be free from want?

- I really know. It's a question I never asked myself. Perhaps with fifty, I might take a while.

- Fifty? Very well. I want them to bring by Marta.

- It's nice of you, he said. I knew you were a Queen, but there... He thought reach 50,000 dollars in appreciation of the letters that he addressed her for weeks.

- But be careful what you make with Marta. I'm not sharing. From now on, you must book your affection for me! "

Griselda was open and direct. She knew by experience that the mules were often mistresses of those for whom they worked. But Charles understood the warning. He will stop any relationship with Marta and reserves for what he considered a Queen. For which favor he could hope of better.

Finally, it was not Marta who took him the requested fifty. She was asked to change the neighborhood. It was Gabriel who came to see him. But unlike what Charles Cosby was expected, it was not to bring her 50,000 dollars as he thought. It was fifty kilos of cocaine which were handed. What to earn much more than his rocks of Crack. He knew then that if he managed to sell them without getting caught, it was assured fortune. He stopped so the Crack and became the main dealer of cocaine in his neighborhood. With what it would bring him, he was able to hold a good year and provide his mother with whom he lived, everything she had ever known.

The following week, he returned to the prison. Griselda had asked him to bring 5,000 dollars to give to the Chief. He gave him the envelope at the same time as the form, and when he went into the visiting room, he understood what this money was used. They were all alone. And given perfume smell that exuded Griselda, she had planned to do something else to discuss. He was hardly closely to her, she threw herself on him and undressed him without that he sketched the slightest

149

reaction. It was their first one cavorts. But who says former says short. They began necessarily again a second time with the same intensity. They settled just a short break, time to catch their breath, and decided to finish in ecstasy by a third time.

"I want that whenever you come to me, you give me so much pleasure, she whispered in ear.

- I will, my Queen, you can trust me! "

My queen! This is very long that a man not told her this way. Griselda who believed herself immune against love, who thought he could never fall in love, forever untied the affections and feelings, felt that something was happening. She even forgot to that men were more prey, just good to give her pleasure.

On leaving prison, Charles Cosby went home in struggling. He had not planned such a use of energy. Everything as he had not planned to make love and so took no condom. He said that on his side, he risked nothing because she was in jail and there were only women behind the walled enclosure. She no longer risked nothing. Yet, this had not stopped him for as much. And they had made three times love.

The next day, his provider returned with fifty other pounds. Despite the pleasure that it gave him, he found it embarrassing because he had not finished to set off the first delivery. He therefore had to think how to sell as many goods. As if the following week, we took it to him so much, there could no longer store it where. He had to step it up a notch if he wanted to take as many goods. He had no choice. Gone are the days of the small-time drug dealer who was selling in his neighborhood. He had to take the high ground. He then proceeded in connection with his knowledge and promised them the fortune in exchange for a pact of solidarity.

"Each of you will receive an amount that he must sell. Just of what deale in your neighborhood. Do not risk take. Half of the recipe will be for you and the other for me. And whenever you bring her me, I'll give you another quantity of powder to sell. We always find ourselves in a street corner or in a bar. Never at my place or yours. Right? »

His new friends were able to only accept. How to refuse such a real bargain. The network of Charles Cosby was immediately set up. And it worked so that all began to want more goods. So much more than other young people of the neighborhood wanted, too, to crunch it.

"Are there not for everyone, guys. Then to you to choose. Or we stay like that and you're just what we win, or we become greedy and we take more risk. Are you willing to risk to go to jail? "

The threat of jail then cooled their ardor. After all, they had not intended to get rich but to earn enough money to live better without having to get up every morning to work hard and earn poverty wages.

A month after the start of his new business, Charles Cosby made the accounts. He had passed two hundred kilos of cocaine and earned a half-million dollars. He had accumulated so much money in cash in his room that he had to buy a safe to store his bundles of bills. On the advice of his mother, who was alarmed when install this chest, he opened a bank account in the same agency of her and laid ten thousand dollars. And a week later, he deposited ten thousand other dollars but, this time, on it of his mother. While I'm glad that his son makes a good life, she knew that the money came from drugs. Because only drug related so much money. But she had missed so much, decided to close their eyes. Even though she knew it would end badly. As he had asked his mother to open another account in another bank.

«I don't know how long my business is going to last, Mom, he said one day when he noticed that his mother did not leave eyes. But I want more you find in misery. So every month, you're going to open an account in a different Bank and we will deposit it $ 10,000.

- You make so much money, my son? She ventured to ask him, still worried.

- I could buy a big car as make all dealers. But me, Mom, it's not my type. All that interests me, is that we are never in misery.

- It's dangerous, my son, you know? You're not afraid that the police arrest you and put you in prison?

-Don't worry, Mom, I'm careful. And anyway, no matter what happens to me. As long as I know that you are free from want and if someday you're sick, you'll have enough money to make you care, I will have accomplished my role of son. " These remarks, instead of reassuring his mother, had the merit of being clear.

And the business continued. And they marched so Charles continued to earn money. And more and more.

On its side, his prison visits went better and better. The chief guardian even had them available to a closed room so they can give free rein to their romps without having to hold back for fear of being seen. This place was kind of a room in a room that was usually used to store cleaning products. It was this so they rave about in peace.

Thanking him for the pleasure he gave her, Griselda made Charles Cosby her representative exclusive. She sent him on a mission across the country to meet his henchmen. A luxury for him who had never left his neighborhood of Oakland. And he took taste to these trips, becoming the same supplier by delivering the goods which intermediaries entrusted him. And for each parcel delivery, given an envelope of $ 1 million which 20% came back to him. He, who so far had failed everything, who had never had more than a few tens of dollars in the hands, that's millions were piling up. He found himself with piles of bills in their pockets. He bought a bigger safe, which had the result of worry a little more his poor mother. Finally, poor mother who now was far from poor. In fact, she filed weekly money accordingly in multiple bank accounts she owned. But by spirit of consciousness, she continued to work.

Charles Cosby was no longer happy. He had become rich to millions, and his mother was immune to the need until the end of her days. No matter what will happen now, he had an easy conscience. Even if the money he earned was the fruit of drug trafficking that led to a terrible human misery. What is more, Griselda gave him more important missions. And he fulfills his role, she wanted to give him so well promoted. She asked him to ensure the effectiveness of the network of distributors. Each of his visits to the prison, after having satisfied his sexual appetite and he had to make her an account in good standing and bring her all the discrepancies.

But the task was arduous and a weekly visit is no longer enough to ensure the right direction of the network. They decided to organize daily telephone conversations speaking in coded language, because they knew that they were listened to. At these discussions that a layman wouldn't understand, they added daily and coded correspondence, she also. This allowed to address all the problems and transform the weekly visit to a sort of briefing devoted to quench their sexual appetites and to organize the work of Charles for the coming week.

Things happened for the better until the American president Georges Bush, declares war on cocaine trafficking. The gossips said while this determination of the president came to him of an arrest of his son, Georges Walter, in 1972, in possession of bags of cocaine. The fact is that the DEA, the Narcotic Bureau and the FBI received for priority mission to put an end to cartels that produced the white powder in Colombia. And the most important of these cartels was this of Medellin.

In Colombia, the victims of the drug war was worthy of a true civil war figures. Dozens of judges, hundreds of journalists and politicians, thousands of police and soldiers had been murdered. In nearly six years of conflict with the Power, the Medellin cartel had killed nearly 10,000 people. Thanks to their financial power, estimated as important as American major companies such Coca-Cola, IBM and General Motors, their drug money, that some called

"Pedrodollars", they had a real army serving them with a thousand men determined.

The Colombian State had not yielded so far. Even after the attack of the Palace of justice in Bogota in 1985 by a group of guerrillas, M-19, which had destroyed the main building and caused the death of half of the judges of the Supreme Court and a hundred auxiliaries of justice, police and military. Terror moved in the country and the murder of the Chief of police and the Minister of justice in Bogota, had plunged the country into chaos. Members of the cartel had found their slogan "Plata o Plomo", silver or lead. And finally to convince the undecided, they had proposed to the Colombian Government to pay the external debt of the country to the International Monetary Front in exchange for their impunity. Either the equivalent of $ 11 billion. Of what to be cold in the back.

This war was compared to the "Violencia", the civil war, which lasted from 1948 to 1957 and had nearly three hundred thousand dead. As these criminals dare to go to a State, to the same level as these bands of guerrillas who delivered a war of so-called liberation.

At the end of the civil war of the 'Violencia', a national front, led by a military junta, had been formed to govern the country. This national front saw Liberals and Conservatives cease their fighting and share power in successive every four years, corresponding to the duration of the presidential mandate, without letting other political groups stand for the presidential elections. So that left supporters were more than armed struggle to challenge this power-sharing. In 1960, the men regrouped to form M-19, ELN and FARC, Marxist guerrillas supported by the Colombian Communist

Party and decided to confront the Colombian army. In 1965, the policy response was to authorize the Department of war to help the formation of paramilitary groups of the right-wing, the paramilitaries United of Colombia, AUC, and the Black Eagles, in Tolima and Llanos, regions of the eastern where the biggest landowners. This political order lasted until 1989, date on which it was declared unconstitutional by the Supreme Court of Justice.

This latent civil war allowed to occupy military forces and promote the existence of drug traffickers who went not without to fund these clashes allowing them to go to their traffic with impunity. At least until the fall of the Berlin wall and the end of Soviet power which reoriented the political priorities of United States who then turned to their neighbors of America. The Colombian authorities were waiting for it and called to help their neighbor to the North, United States of America.

A huge media campaign was launched to raise awareness. Many stakeholders, politicians, journalists, sports, film and music personalities, demanded the launching of actions to eradicate drug trafficking that was destroying youth. In this issue, a prohibitionist policy was set up, accompanied by severe penal measures and the aggravation of penalties floors which caused an explosion in the prison population. The most committed asked what a real war is delivered to drug traffickers who inoculated what they called Cancer to the young Americans. Or even to youth in many countries, victims of this scourge compared to AIDS. And they got rich on the misfortune of youth and were waging a war to the first democracy in South

America. An interview of the Colombian president was placed in the loop on all American TV stations.

The president César Gaviria asked American citizens to give up to a vice which enriches criminals and allowed them to threaten democracy in his country. A summit meeting was held in the United Nations Headquarters in New York. Nearly eighty countries signed a Pact to put their resources to combat drug trafficking and money laundering.

The first consequence was to declare criminal those States whose leaders brought their support to drug traffickers. In December 1990, the American army intervened to Panama to capture the Panamanian dictator Manuel Noriega, actor in international cocaine trafficking. Economic sanctions were then decreed against States that were not effectively fighting drug traffickers. The Bolivian dictator Luis Garcia Tajada, was clearly targeted. The president Jaime Zamora, who succeeded him, extradited to United State Luis Arce Gomez, the former Minister of the Interior of the former dictator, accused of drug trafficking. Other leaders rebelling against what they called imperialist, arguing that those responsible for trafficking in cocaine were not producers of the coca leaf, whose culture was ancestral, but American consumers who sniffed this derivative was cocaine.

Only Mexico and Colombia, in fight against the drug cartels, not opposed. Colombia agreed to two things: the implementation of the law on extradition signed in 1981, repeatedly questioned, and the presence of agents of DEA in their national territory.

The Government of Washington, who made the priority of priorities, provided the sum of eight billion dollars at the request of president Georges Bush, to finance his war against drug trafficking. Tens of millions of military equipment were delivered to the army and the Colombian police to carry its fight against militias private of the cartels.

The heads of the cartels, who were not afraid of the armed struggle, then saw him show up the worst of the threats: that of extradition. They decreed a total war against the Colombian Government, that he cancels this extradition treaty in arguing that they prefer a grave in Colombia rather than a prison cell in United States. They then began a fight to the death and is surrounded by an army of professionals of the guerrillas, including many foreigners.

But after years of open war, the leaders of the Medellin cartel were no longer in situation to fight effectively. The actions of the Colombian Government, aided by United States, will eventually push them towards the abyss. The Medellin cartel, whose leaders had been killed and others surrendered in exchange of the immunity, no longer existed. Only Pablo Escobar Gaviria clung to his Machiavellian empire. But his days were numbered.

Griselda was concerned. She worried a lot. Since her falling out with the Ochoa family, her both sons were put at the service of the head of the Medellin cartel. And by the time running, she had reason to be worried because news from the country was far from good. To such point that this had to happen, happened. Osvaldo, the youngest of the three sons she had with Carlos Trujillo, was killed by a commando of four men in the center of Medellin.

When she learned the news by her mother, Griselda was a great sadness. But she was just sad. A desire to revenge submerged her. But she did not know where to turn. Then, she spoke to Charles Cosby that he intervenes before Jorge Riverito Ayala. He would find her son's killers. She asked him to make sure to find his killers and make them pay dear, very dear, this act. She wanted them to suffer as they had never suffered.

An investigation was immediately launched to find the men who killed Osvaldo. And she advanced quickly even as the killers, sure of their impunity, had not even hidden face to commit their crime. The men who were looking for them began only two weeks to find their traces. And to answer the request of Griselda, the killers were cut in pieces and the rests of their bodies were lined up along a road to let everyone know what it cost when we dared go to the family of Griselda Blanco.

END OF REIGN

But everything has an end. Pablo Escobar Gaviria was found by the Colombian policemen of elite in the Los Olivos district and killed on December 2, 1993. The one who headed the Medellin cartel was finally dead. And those who worked alongside him were also bewildered that lost. The demand for cocaine, she did not give so far. Then for the dealers of the whole world, a problem arose. There were many Cali cartel who also produced tons of cocaine. But this one wanted to know nothing about those who tampered with Pablo Escobar Gaviria, the criminal with whom they were in war. They had yet provided the networks those of Medellin provided more but now, things were different. They knew that they were now the masters of the game and wanted to impose their conditions on those who wanted to buy cocaine.

All of the world's mafias were desperate. They had yet to find a solution to find suppliers. We spoke to them then the FARC, the Marxist militias, that were fighting against the power of Bogota and who financed their guerrilla with drug trafficking. An approach was tried and things went rather well because these guerrillas were a boon that the Cali cartel wants to limit the number of its customers. The leaders of the FARC agreed to make business with those who could not provide in Cali. International traffic could resume.

In United States, things were different. The stream passing through Miami had fallen in the hands of the men of the Cali cartel. Griselda's men had to find another door of entry. Too bad for Florida. After all, it wasn't the ports that were missing in United States.

But the DEA agents remained not inactive and continued their war against drug traffickers. They took advantage of the rivalry between the Colombian, who was speaking in shots of machine-guns, to play on this table and obtain information. The head of the network of Griselda, Jorge Riverito Ayala was arrested after being given by informants at the orders of the Cali cartel.

The DEA agents showed him things; participation in drug trafficking: 30 years in prison. Murders of 120 people: life in prison multiplied by the number of homicides. What was that he should live as long as Methuselah to hope out of prison alive. But as he was an important figure, he was offered a deal: he was delivering his network, indicating forces details, and he could benefit from the program of protection of witnesses. All his crimes would be forgotten and he could continue to live free under a new identity. Jorge Riverito Ayala hesitated less than a minute before deciding and sat down. He gave all the information asked: starting with the names of the men who worked for him.

The judicial case against Griselda Blanco is expanded. It was time to judge the 'Cocaine Queen' for the murders. He had to say that they were numerous and had filled the obituaries of newspapers for years. The journalists were informed by officers who needed the indignation of public opinion to make the sentence that they wanted, namely the death penalty.

You then spoke of the murder of a couple, Alfredo and Graziella Lorenzo, who had bought five kilos of cocaine to Griselda Blanco and owed her two hundred fifty thousand dollars. As they had taken time to honor their debt, she had sent Jorge Riverito Ayala to punish them. The killer had quietly entered in their Florida villa and had killed them while their three children were quietly installed in the living room watching television. They had realized nothing and had discovered the bodies of their parents lying in their bed.

But the crime that rebelled most the public opinion was this one of a child of two years, Johnny Castro. His father, Jesus Chucho Castro, was one of the many bodyguards of Griselda Blanco and, one day, he provided oversight of Michael Corleone, he dared give him a kick in the butt, infuriated by the whims of the boy. When she had learned that her blood had put a tour. She had called Jorge Riverito Ayala, alone in which she had confidence and had asked him to punish him in the worst of ways. He had immediately set out hunting but had to take precautions because the man, who had known that his gesture was not forgiven by the 'Cocaine Queen', flew from his home and had hired some bodyguards armed, he too.

It took several days for Jorge Riverito Ayala to track him down and put him under surveillance in an attempt to kill him without being exposed to retaliation from his door-guns. The opportunity arose a few days later while Jesus Chucho Castro riding in town with his car, feeling safe surrounded by his bodyguards. But he had forgotten the audacity of the "Cocaine Cowboys". They chased after the car, reached its height and opened fire on the vehicle before fleeing. The car made a swerve and ended his race against a fire hydrant. The police intervened after a few minutes and made the finding of the strafing: Jesus

Chucho Castro was wounded by two bullets; two of his bodyguards were killed, but worse everything, her child, Johnny, who was at his side, had been hit by the burst which was to kill his father. The child came to be the first collateral victim of Miami where the war between drug traffickers was incessant.

When she learned the consequence of this ambush, Griselda Blanco spurred an angry because Jesus Chucho Castro was still alive. But when she learned that his son of two year old had been killed, so she merely say to Jorge Riverito Ayala: "like this, Castro and me, we're even."

The revelation of this heinous crime revolted the public opinion which claimed that those who committed this heinous crime deserve only punishment: death.

In front of the many revelations of Jorge Riverito Ayala, the Prosecutor of the Prosecutor's office of Florida edited an extradition order to the Governor of California who, before the pressure of the public opinion, was able to accept her transfer. The operation was entrusted to the Sergeant Al Singleton, Chief of the Centac 26, a special force formed to fight against the drug cartels which spread out in Florida. The brigade then flew to San Francisco, was lend armoured vehicles, and went to prison. In the office of the Director, Al Singleton presented to Griselda Blanco the extradition order for Miami-Dade where she would be tried for the murder of three people: Alfredo and Graziella Lorenzo and Johnny Castro. She was taken immediately to nausea and vomiting because she knew she risked the death penalty. It seems that the account of the 'Cocaine Queen' was settled.

A few days later, Charles Cosby, he too, found himself under fire from the current events. He received a summons so that he appears in the office of the Judge of Miami-Dade District. Not knowing why he was summoned, he stood alone and without a lawyer. A boon for the judge, who informed him that he was the subject of a survey about drug trafficking. To make him talk, the judge reminded him the penalties for drug traffickers. And finally to convince him, the police showed him photos where he appeared with men suspected of drug trafficking.

Charles fell from the clouds. On the pictures they showed him, he lives a part of the men who worked for him. "How this was possible without that he doesn't know what?" He asked himself. That the photos filed and he was overwhelmed by panic. But he checked himself and confessed nothing. "Yes, he knew his men and after?" He told to the judge. He was then asked to think carefully because when the evidence of his guilt would be proven, he would end his life in jail. And it would be too late to accept the market officers proposed him.

He went out two hours later from the judge's office and went directly to the prison where he came to seek advice from Griselda. He told him what the judge told him.

"It's Jorge Riverito who headed the network and making the link between everybody. He was him my right-hand man, she told him. If ever he tell everything, that is the end of our organization!

- They got us not, honey, muttered Charles.

- By going out from here, I want you to find the best lawyers. It doesn't matter how much it will cost! They must take care of us and defend us at all costs. It is the only way for you to avoid the life imprisonment! "

The legal maneuvers began. And the DEA investigations resumed as Jorge Riverito Ayala, after his confidences and delivered some information to lock out Griselda Blanco in Miami-Dade, now he refused to talk. He knew that if he spoke, even with the law of protection of witnesses, he would never be safe. And above all, his family living in Colombia would pay the price of his betrayal. And he did not want his pay for him. Then, he was in hiding in the most complete dumbness. But DEA, which had completed its investigation, launched court proceedings. Jorge Riverito Ayala and his accomplices were able to be accused of abuses they had committed for years. Things looked good and the trial could not only lead to the result that Robert Palombo hoped for so long. The 'Cocaine Queen' would end her life on death row.

We were in 1999. The trial began. But now FBI released an information which crippled the trial. Griselda Blanco, who could no longer stay in prison, had considered as friends of the Medellin cartel kidnapping John-John Kennedy, the son of the former President, in 1995 to negotiate an exchange between him and her. Charles Cosby was this one who planned the operation. But had deflated, saying that he would give nothing. Griselda had yet insisted. But nothing was done. He had not conducted this crazy project by explaining he didn't have the skills to make it. Decided to continue, she then asked him to get in touch with her eldest son, Dixon, who he would because he had participated in many kidnappings on behalf of Pablo Escobar Gaviria.

Dixon, the eldest son of Griselda, had left Colombia after the murder of his younger brother, Osvaldo. The madness of Pablo Escobar Gaviria ended disgust, and he felt that this paranoia would, too, in the grave. He had been this one who had established the first contacts with the Cali cartel on behalf of his mother after his falling out with the Ochoa family. Then, it was even him who had taken in relation to some leaders of FARC to get goods. Once the network in place, he had designated a representative on site then took the plane to United States where he had taken refuge in New York, taking a new name and settling in a neighborhood where he felt safe because he had many friends. Once on the spot, he was then began to organize the kidnapping of the son of the former American president.

For his part, Charles Cosby, scalded by his visit to the judge and who felt that things took a bad turn, began to take distance and tried to organize the traffic in his own way. He knew now that he was being watched closely by the police. He needed so play tight and exercise the greatest caution. But after failing to kidnap John-John Kennedy, he knew that he had to show credentials and make something so that Griselda keeps him her confidence. He knew what she was capable and this made him more afraid than prison. He had thought of an ingenious idea and then proposed a plan that, after talking to his lawyers, put an end to any legal action.

The trial began, under a strong media mediatization, and the accusations against Griselda Blanco began and

166

squeezed in the course of days, taking a threatening form. She risked the death penalty for three murders for which we blamed her. But now that Charles Cosby intervened. He asked to be auditioned and confessed to the judge having had sexual relations with one of the secretaries of the Prosecutor. Jorge Riverito Ayala, him, had had Phone sexual relations with two other Secretaries when he was auditioned by the services of DEA. It is true that the man had a charm to which it was not resisting.

The press took information and the scandal that broke out was worse than anything. The three women were forced to resign. The judge, Katherine Fernandez Rundle, who hoped to take advantage of the media impact to promote her career, felt ridiculed publicly and sought to negotiate with lawyers of Griselda Blanco to end as quickly as possible, at the trial which took a bizarre turn.

The lawyers, who knew that they had won, agreed to negotiate but demanded that their client benefits an unconditional release in 2004. This was due to the fact that his condemnation to three sentences of twenty years prison, cannot be combined because Griselda Blanco had pleaded guilty, had been achieved for a third. The judge gave his approval but, as he needed all similarly get a success if she didn't want to be the target of the press, announced that, immediately after his release, Griselda Blanco would be extradited and sent back to Colombia with a ban on vacation to life in United States.

The agreement was concluded and accepted by Griselda Blanco, who in addition to being satisfied with the outcome, learned that Jorge Riverito Ayala, him, would have no amnesty and would be charged for these three murders. He escaped the death penalty but was sentenced to three prison sentences for life.

Law on unconditional release had been decreed by the American Government in the mid-1990s. To effectively fight drug trafficking, the American Federal authorities had offered to traffickers who delivered information, unconditional freedom and extradition to their countries of origin. The agreement had been difficult to negotiate with the Colombian authorities, who saw a dim view of hundreds of traffickers back to the country and put themselves at the service of the cartels that they were fighting. But the Colombian Government had eventually given insofar as she broke the Treaty of extradition of Colombian traffickers sought by American justice. It was a ready for rendering.

Robert Palombo, the man who had devoted his life to fighting against the "Cocaine Queen" was a slight pinch in the heart by watching the plane take off. He knew that inside was this woman of 1 meter 52, who did shake Miami for years, and that he had ten years before being able to put her in prison. Failing to have condemned her to death, he knew that with more than two hundred and fifty murders under her belt, she wouldn't have to old bones. After all, she would only have to be resent her even. He knew that in Colombia, she had left too many dead bodies behind her to avoid the revenge of the friends or relatives of her victims. Including the Ochoa brothers who wanted her head for years and were ready to everything to make her pay the death of their cousin.

EPILOGUE

The plane of Avianca Company landed on the tarmac of the Eldorado-Bogotá airport. We were in August 2005. Griselda Blanco, wearing with simple jeans and a vulgar cotton blouse, went out of the unit watching people activate. She expected the worst host committees. Walking through the alleys of the airport, she lives busy people come and go. She couldn't help but smile. How many of them were mules carrying drugs in their intestines. As it was now the fashionable way to pass customs controls without getting sniffed by dogs of the customs.

The years spent behind the gates of the prison had had a devastating effect on Griselda. They gave her the look of a woman of her age. A woman approaching sixty. As in prison, the luxury of massages, beauty treatments, sessions whit the hairdresser. Her hair had a funny appearance. In addition to grey, they were sparse, as if she was bald.

Meanwhile, Griselda was on her guard. She knew as American justice had failed to pass on the Chair electric for the murders, or did commit, the best way to make her go away was back home, in Colombia, where others would take care of it. So, she expected at any time to see a man with a gun out and shoot her. And at point-blank range to be sure not to miss her. Then, she skirted the walls and advanced as far as the outside, looking around and chooses a taxi, not without making sure that the driver had a good head.

"Take me to the bus station! She said in a firm tone.

She looked out of the window as the cab progressed in the maze of streets, plagued by traffic jams. She was surprised by the number of new buildings for the most part, what she saw. The capital was developed in an incredible pace. "The drug money does not benefit just to the traffickers", she thought. But it was true that this was more than twenty years she had not returned in Colombia. This dates back to the time when she came to settle the account of her ex-husband, Alberto Bravo. Besides, she remembered that she was without news of her eldest son, Dixon. She knew he was hiding in United States, but she had to find him.

Griselda arrived ten hours later in Medellin. She had forgotten how much these coach journeys were painful. She had done a few with her Alberto yet. But that was another era. At the bus station, she took a taxi and went to the El Poblado district, a few blocks from the Monaco Building that Pablo Escobar Gaviria had bought to hide with his family. It was there that the Cali cartel, with who he was in war, blew a car full of dynamite. In this secure subdivision where we entered only after showing his identity to two armed guards guarding the grid access, she did buy a villa. She had bought this luxurious house in this place because she knew that most of his neighbors were officers of the police or the army, magistrates or judges, officials or politicians. She knew that here, she would be safe from any threat.

She, who had spent years locked in a cell of 9 square meters, could appreciate to settle in a villa of 250 square meters with a heated pool, a sauna, and amenities to make your life easier.

Griselda showed her passport to the guard who addressed her a smile of welcome. He looked at her with attention, being interested in the funny look of this woman who did not seem like much, and he wished to have a nice day by returning her his passport having made sure of her identity. A new life was waiting for Griselda Blanco. A life like she had more known since his departure precipitated of Miami. Besides, the first thing she had planned to make was to spend two hours in a good hot bath, in order to get rid of any dirt accumulated during her years in prison, where only a shower for a few minutes per week was authorized. And after being washed and lively, she would bring a hairdresser at home to make her a nice haircut. The life had to take back its rights.

And this life continued, without problem until 2007 where Michael Corleone came to see her. Ana Lucia was dead and he had made to repatriate her body so that he is buried in Medellin. The steps had been complex but he managed because he knew that he would greatly please to her mother. In exchange, he asked council because he too, wanted to engage in cocaine trafficking as demand was still not down. His mother gave him so his advice but warned: "it's a world where you can't trust anyone. You know my son." After a few days spent together, she took back him up to the airport of Bogota.

What she didn't know yet, is that she doesn't see him again. Not more than Dixon who was now hiding in the jungle where he joined the FARC, which exported bulk drugs to finance their war. His knowledge in this area had allowed him to get a high position and responsibilities. But he called Dixon Bravo, of the name of his father.

In may 2012, Griselda learned through his lawyers that his son, Michael Corleone Sepúlveda, came to be arrested in Miami for drug trafficking. She knew what he could and asked them to do their utmost to avoid too heavy prison sentence.

But she wouldn't see the progress of the trial.

A few months later, on Monday, 3 September, Griselda Blanco decided to leave her secure residence, for the first time in months. She was going to have 70 years and had decided to take a last walk in the city. She longed to Enchiladas and wanted to buy the meat to make them prepared by his cook. She ordered a taxi who laid her in front of the butcher of Medellin who was best known.

She alighted from the taxi and walked on the sidewalk. She was a few meters from the butcher shop when a motorcycle resulted in the street. Two men were on it. She heard the sound of the engine and turned. She was not afraid because she had guessed that these men were there for her. It was she who had imported this way of killing in Miami. A method that was raging in the dark hours of the Medellin cartel.

When the bike was in front of her, she looked at those who drove her. She was not afraid and preferred to look death in the face. She recovered the film of her life, her moments of sadness and misfortune, and the moments where she had known love and happiness. She who had refused all morality and had lived without any morality. But her life was imbued with adventures and a heavy dose of pepper. She was proud of it and had no regrets. If things were to do it again, she would remake them. And with the same pleasure. As his fate was unique.

Two shots slammed and blew up the skull. He was fifteen hours and the death had just caught up her.

CPSIA information can be obtained
at www.ICGtesting.com
Printed in the USA
LVHW052144161120
671836LV00016B/2700

9 781974 467778